Soft Skills
for the Workplace

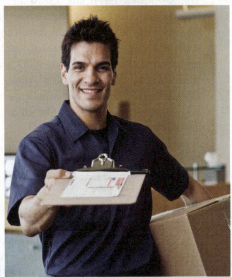

Publisher
The Goodheart-Willcox Company, Inc.
Tinley Park, IL
www.g-w.com

The Goodheart-Willcox Company, Inc. Brand Disclaimer: Brand names, company names, and illustrations for products and services included in this text are provided for educational purposes only and do not represent or imply endorsement or recommendation by the author or the publisher.

The Goodheart-Willcox Company, Inc. Safety Notice: The reader is expressly advised to carefully read, understand, and apply all safety precautions and warnings described in this book or that might also be indicated in undertaking the activities and exercises described herein to minimize risk of personal injury or injury to others. Common sense and good judgment should also be exercised and applied to help avoid all potential hazards. The reader should always refer to the appropriate manufacturer's technical information, directions, and recommendations; then proceed with care to follow specific equipment operating instructions. The reader should understand these notices and cautions are not exhaustive.

The publisher makes no warranty or representation whatsoever, either expressed or implied, including but not limited to equipment, procedures, and applications described or referred to herein, their quality, performance, merchantability, or fitness for a particular purpose. The publisher assumes no responsibility for any changes, errors, or omissions in this book. The publisher specifically disclaims any liability whatsoever, including any direct, indirect, incidental, consequential, special, or exemplary damages resulting, in whole or in part, from the reader's use or reliance upon the information, instructions, procedures, warnings, cautions, applications, or other matter contained in this book. The publisher assumes no responsibility for the activities of the reader.

The Goodheart-Willcox Company, Inc. Internet Disclaimer: The Internet resources and listings in this Goodheart-Willcox Publisher product are provided solely as a convenience to you. These resources and listings were reviewed at the time of publication to provide you with accurate, safe, and appropriate information. Goodheart-Willcox Publisher has no control over the referenced websites and, due to the dynamic nature of the Internet, is not responsible or liable for the content, products, or performance of links to other websites or resources. Goodheart-Willcox Publisher makes no representation, either expressed or implied, regarding the content of these websites, and such references do not constitute an endorsement or recommendation of the information or content presented. It is your responsibility to take all protective measures to guard against inappropriate content, viruses, or other destructive elements.

Cover images: Rawpixel.com/Shutterstock.com, Monkey Business Images/Shutterstock.com, ESB Essentials/Shutterstock.com, michaeljung/Shutterstock.com, AVAVA/Shutterstock.com

Case Study background image: Toria/Shutterstock.com

Library of Congress Cataloging-in-Publication Data

Names: Goodheart-Willcox Company, issuing body.
Title: Soft skills for the workplace.
Description: First edition. | Tinley Park, IL : Goodheart-Willcox Company, Inc., [2018] | Includes index.
Identifiers: LCCN 2016046673 | ISBN 9781631268267
Subjects: LCSH: Vocational guidance. | Soft skills. | Vocational qualifications.
Classification: LCC HF5381 .S644 2018 | DDC 650.1--dc23 LC record available at https://lccn.loc.gov/2016046673

Preface

Soft Skills for the Workplace is an overview of basic behaviors, etiquette, and protocol that a career-minded person needs in order to communicate effectively as a professional. Soft skills are the employability skills that help an individual find a job, perform well in the workplace, and gain success in a job or career. In today's workplace, employers look for people who have job-specific skills to perform on the job as well as the know-how to interact with coworkers and customers. You may be the most qualified person in your field in terms of hard skills, but if you lack soft skills, you may have a challenge finding and retaining employment.

Soft Skills for the Workplace presents the important interpersonal skills requested by today's employers. Presented in one easy-to-use text, your students will learn the basic soft skills needed for career success. There is no need for multiple references to introduce students to employability skills when using this unique text. Suitable for any class or discipline, each chapter can be used as a supplemental conversation starter or as an independent assignment for students. When the course has concluded, the text can serve as a personal reference for students to use as they develop their careers.

The modular format of the content provides flexibility to assign topics in the order that adapts to your curriculum. Fourteen short, concise chapters provide information that prepares students to maximize and refine their talents. A chapter-opening soft skills quiz or video sets the stage for the content that follows. End-of-chapter activities provide opportunities for self-assessment as well as additional practice activities on the G-W Learning companion website.

By studying *Soft Skills for the Workplace*, students will gain understanding of the value of mastering the art of professionalism for their chosen career. Learning how to embrace and apply accepted workplace protocol is a first step toward personal success. *Soft skills* are the new *hard skills* for the 21st century.

Additional Resources

The G-W Learning companion website is a free student resource that provides additional study materials in an interactive electronic format. Data files for the soft skills practice activities at the end of each chapter may be downloaded and completed for additional practice. Also included on the website are pretests, posttests, videos, and vocabulary activities that complement selected chapters. The website is located at **www.g-wlearning.com/careereducation/**

G-W's instructor resources include everything you need to utilize *Soft Skills for the Workplace* in your classroom. A variety of materials are provided on the Instructor's Resource CD to help you make the most of information needed to teach each chapter, such as answer keys and instructional strategies. For your convenience, lesson plans and activity solutions are also included.

Acknowledgments

Goodheart-Willcox Publisher would like to thank the following individuals for their honest and valuable input in the development of the first edition of *Soft Skills for the Workplace*.

David L. Batts, Associate Professor, East Carolina University–College of Engineering and Technology, Greenville, NC

Deborah Boone, Department Chair, School of Business, Halifax Community College, Weldon, NC

Amy Burns, Experiential Learning Program Coordinator, Northwestern Michigan College, Traverse City, MI

Cindi Hanna, Program Coordinator/Data Analyst, Forsyth Technical Community College, Winston-Salem, NC

Dan Humpert, Associate Professor Emeritus, University of Cincinnati, College of Engineering and Applied Science, Cincinnati, OH

Julia A. Hollins, Ed.D./ET, CEO-School Administrator, JH Virtual Business Services, Inc. online school, Atlanta, GA

Mary E. Koval, M.A., Sociology, Career Development, Diversity, and Group Dynamics Instructor, Bryant and Stratton College, North Chesterfield, VA

Joe Moore, Automotive Instructor/Associate Professor, Southern Maine Community College, South Portland, ME

Brian Noel, Automotive Mechanics Technology Professor, Cosumnes River College, Sacramento, CA

Micheal L. Randolph, MS, RMA, Instructor, Medical Assisting, Gateway Tech College, Racine, WI

Traci Robinson, Curriculum Specialist, Butler Technology & Career Development Schools, Hamilton, OH

Ethan Robles, Assistant Director of Admission, Lafayette College, Easton, PA

Paul D. Shuler, Ph.D., Director, Academic Quality & Workforce, Texas Higher Education Coordinating Board, Austin, TX

Jason Slade, Faculty/Engineering Technology, Northwestern Michigan College, Traverse City, MI

Travis Southerland, HVAC Instructor, Southern Oklahoma Technology Center, Ardmore, OK

Beryl Alli Vainshtein, MBA, Business Technology Instructor, Saint Paul College, Saint Paul, MN

Michael E. Valdez, Vice Principal Career Technical Education Programs, Career and Technical Education Coordinator, Office of Correctional Education, Sacramento, CA

Brief Contents

CHAPTER 1
Professionalism 1

CHAPTER 2
Ethics 9

CHAPTER 3
Self-Management Skills 19

CHAPTER 4
Etiquette 28

CHAPTER 5
Attire 37

CHAPTER 6
Communication Skills 45

CHAPTER 7
Verbal and Nonverbal Communication 53

CHAPTER 8
Speaking Skills 62

CHAPTER 9
Listening Skills 72

CHAPTER 10
Written Communication 83

CHAPTER 11
Writing and Interviewing for Employment 93

CHAPTER 12
Teams 111

CHAPTER 13
Diversity 120

CHAPTER 14
Confidence 133

APPENDIX A
Punctuation 143
APPENDIX B
Capitalization 147
APPENDIX C
Number Usage 149

Glossary 151
Index 155

Contents

CHAPTER 1
Professionalism 1
- Skills of a Professional 2
  - Hard Skills 2
  - Soft Skills 3
- Positive Attitude 4
- Image of a Professional 5
- CHAPTER REVIEW 6

CHAPTER 2
Ethics 9
- Ethics 10
- Ethical Communication 11
  - Confidentiality 11
  - Social Responsibility 12
- Digital Citizenship 12
  - Intellectual Property 14
  - Copyrights 14
- CHAPTER REVIEW 16

CHAPTER 3
Self-Management Skills 19
- Developing Self-Management Skills 20
  - Emotional Control 20
  - Problem Solving 20
  - Time Management 21
  - Goal Setting 22
- Stress-Management Skills 24
- CHAPTER REVIEW 25

CHAPTER 4
Etiquette 28
- Etiquette 29
- Workspace 30
  - Offices 31
  - Cubicles 31
  - Shared Spaces 32
- Digital Devices 32
- Business Dining 32
- Funerals 33
- CHAPTER REVIEW 34

CHAPTER 5
Attire 37
- Workplace Dress 38
  - Uniforms 38
  - Business-Professional Dress 38
  - Business-Casual Dress 39
  - Jeans Day 39
- Business Meeting Apparel 40
- CHAPTER REVIEW 42

CHAPTER 6
Communication Skills 45
- Communication 46
  - Communication Process 46
  - Communication Barriers 47
- Language 47
  - Condescending Words 49
  - Biased Words 49
  - Jargon and Clichés 49
  - Euphemisms 49
- CHAPTER REVIEW 50

CHAPTER 7
Verbal and Nonverbal Communication 53
- Verbal Communication 54
  - Words 54
  - Voice 54
  - Speaking Situations 55
- Nonverbal Communication 56
  - Body Language 56
  - Eye Contact 57
  - Touch 57
  - Personal Space 57
  - Paralanguage 58
- CHAPTER REVIEW 59

CHAPTER 8
Speaking Skills 62
- Introductions 63
  - Introducing Yourself 63
  - Introducing Others 63
  - Introducing Speakers 64
- Telephone Calls 65
  - Receiving Telephone Calls 65
  - Placing Telephone Calls 66
  - Leaving Voice Mail Messages 66
- Leading a Meeting 67
- CHAPTER REVIEW 69

CHAPTER 9
Listening Skills 72
- Listening Process 73
  - Types of Listening 73
  - Show You are Listening 74

Listen with Purpose 74
   Listen for Specific Information 75
   Listen to Instructions 75
   Listen to Requests 75
   Listen to Persuasive Talk 76
Formal Meetings 77
   Arrive Early 77
   Sit in the Front..77
   Take Notes 77
   Fight Barriers 78
   Provide Feedback 78
   CHAPTER REVIEW 80

CHAPTER 10

Written Communication 83
Writing Etiquette 84
   Letters 84
   E-Mail 87
   Thank-You Notes 89
   RSVP 89
Social Media Etiquette 89
   CHAPTER REVIEW 90

CHAPTER 11

Writing and Interviewing for Employment 93
Résumé, Cover Message, and Portfolio 94
   Résumé 94
   Cover Message 94
   Portfolio 97
Application Process 99
   Applying Online 100
   Applying in Person 100
Preparing for an Interview 100
   Interview Questions 101
   Dress for an Interview 103
After the Interview 104
   Thank-You Message 104
   Interview Evaluation 104
Hiring Process 105
   Employee Checks 105
   Employment Forms 105
   CHAPTER REVIEW 107

CHAPTER 12

Teams 111
Teams in the Workplace 112
   Teamwork 112
   Group Dynamics 113
Conflict Resolution 113

   Difficult People 114
   Leadership 116
   CHAPTER REVIEW 117

CHAPTER 13

Diversity 120
Diversity in the Workplace 121
   Gender 121
   Race 121
   Disability 122
   Age 123
Culture 124
   Cultural Awareness 125
   Cultural Intelligence 126
   Cultural Competency 127
Intercultural Communication 127
   Careful Listening 128
   Clear Speech 128
   Nonverbal Communication 128
Benefits of Diversity 129
   New Ideas 129
   Higher Productivity 129
   Improved Customer Service 129
   Reputation 129
   CHAPTER REVIEW 130

CHAPTER 14

Confidence 133
Self-Confidence 134
Professional Success 135
   Negotiation 135
   Manage Up 136
   Self-Promotion 137
   Office Politics 137
Realistic Expectations 138
   Position 138
   Salary 138
   Benefits 139
   Promotion 139
   CHAPTER REVIEW 140

APPENDIX A

Punctuation 143

APPENDIX B

Capitalization 147

APPENDIX C

Number Usage 149

Glossary 151
Index 155

Focus on Professionalism

Soft Skills for the Workplace will help your students jump-start their career in the competitive work environment of the 21st century. To stand out in the employment crowd and compete for a chosen career, each person entering the workforce must develop essential soft skills.

The unique approach to this text presents content in a format that is condensed, to the point, and can be completed in a brief amount of time. The easy-to-read style and meaningful applications introduce behaviors for successful interactions with employers, coworkers, and customers.

Just the Basics

Each chapter introduces basic soft skills that are needed for career success as recommended by employers. The topics covered are some of the most requested essential workplace skills that can help students develop professionalism and succeed in a chosen career.

Learning Outcomes

At the beginning of each chapter, learning outcomes define the goals that will be accomplished while reading the chapter. Each goal is aligned with the content headings, as well as with the summary at the end of the chapter. The alignment of learning outcomes provides a logical flow through each page of the content so that students may build on individual knowledge as they progress through the chapters.

Before You Read

Each chapter begins with an activity to set the stage for the content to come. Through completion of a pretest in chapter 1, an opportunity is provided for students to evaluate their prior knowledge of soft skills. The chapters that follow include a video to bring realism and provide a relevant connection with content that has been learned. A posttest at the end of the text will help students evaluate what has been learned on completion of the content.

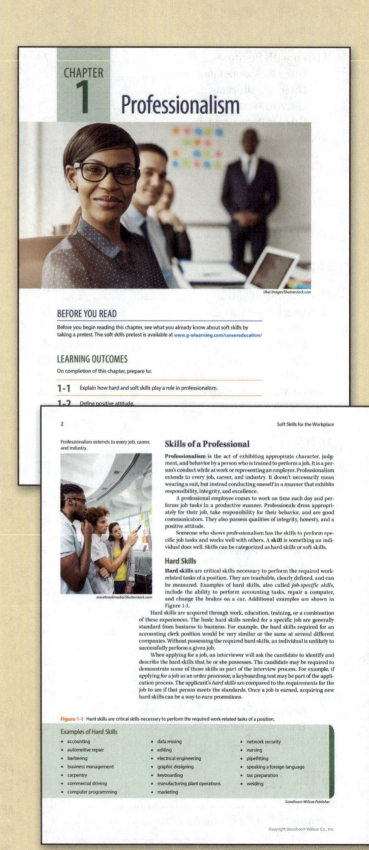

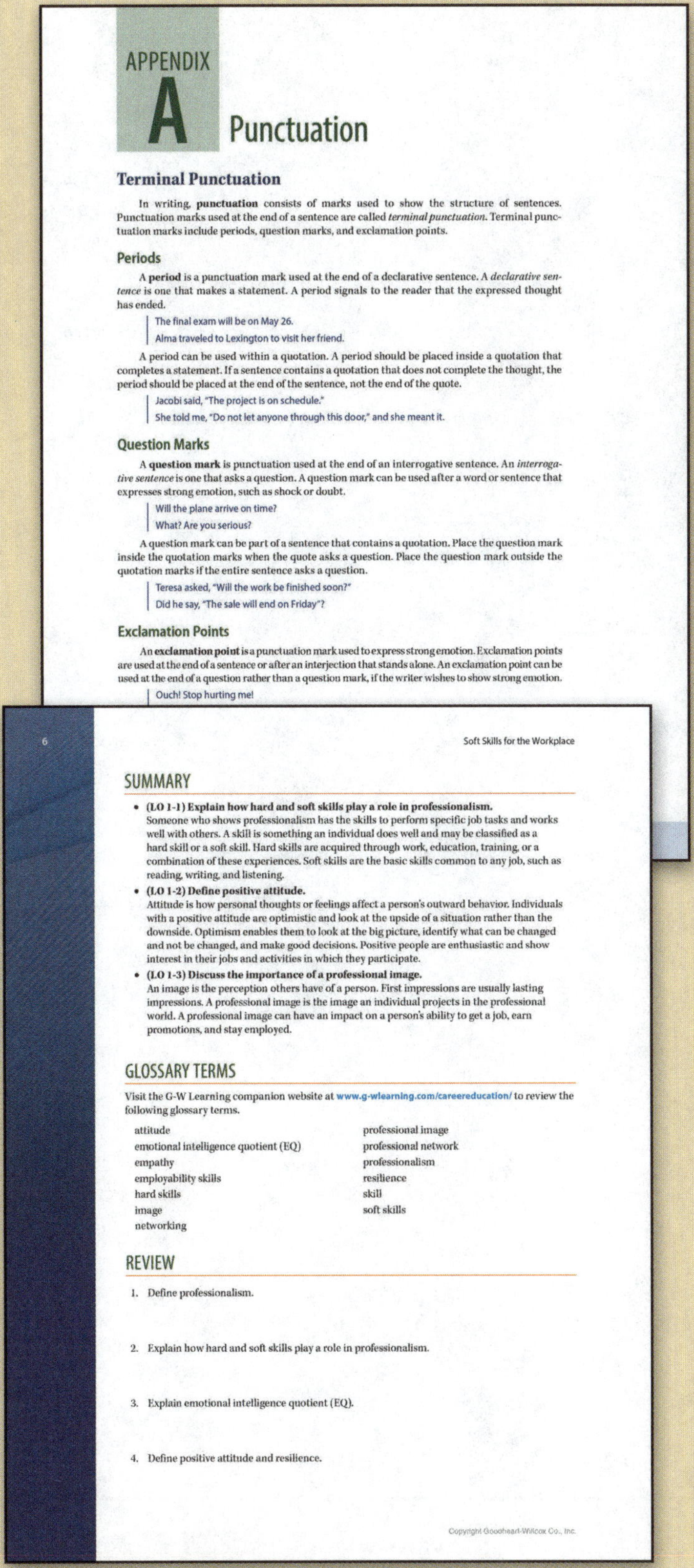

Case Studies

Real-world case studies illustrate the importance of mastering soft skills. Each case includes a workplace situation with questions that provide an opportunity to analyze and summarize opinions, while identifying the soft skills that are addressed.

Appendices

Appendices for punctuation, capitalization, and number usage are included at the end of the text. These appendices highlight grammar mechanics and examples for reference as students complete writing assignments.

End-of-Chapter Content

End-of-chapter material provides opportunity for review and application of concepts.

- A concise **Summary** reiterates the learning outcomes and provides a brief review of the content for student reference.
- **Glossary Terms** identifies important soft skills terms covered in the chapter and listed in the end-of-text glossary.
- **Review** questions highlight basic concepts presented in the chapter so students can evaluate understanding of the material.
- **Application** activities provide an opportunity for self-reflection so students can relate the topics to their personal lives.
- **Internet Activity** exercises provide additional research opportunities for greater understanding of selected concepts discussed in the chapter.
- **Skills Practice** activities provide an opportunity for students to engage in hands-on application of the content to perfect their soft skills. These data files are available for download on the G-W Learning companion website.

G-W Learning Companion Website

The G-W Learning companion website is a free resource that provides additional study materials in an interactive electronic format. Data files for the soft skills practice activities at the end of each chapter may be downloaded and completed for additional practice. Also included on the website are pretests, posttests, and videos that complement selected chapters. The website is located at **www.g-wlearning.com/careereducation/**

The following appears in the sample book page images shown on the left:

APPENDIX A — Punctuation

Terminal Punctuation

In writing, **punctuation** consists of marks used to show the structure of sentences. Punctuation marks used at the end of a sentence are called *terminal punctuation*. Terminal punctuation marks include periods, question marks, and exclamation points.

Periods

A **period** is a punctuation mark used at the end of a declarative sentence. A *declarative sentence* is one that makes a statement. A period signals to the reader that the expressed thought has ended.

> The final exam will be on May 26.
> Alma traveled to Lexington to visit her friend.

A period can be used within a quotation. A period should be placed inside a quotation that completes a statement. If a sentence contains a quotation that does not complete the thought, the period should be placed at the end of the sentence, not the end of the quote.

> Jacobi said, "The project is on schedule."
> She told me, "Do not let anyone through this door," and she meant it.

Question Marks

A **question mark** is punctuation used at the end of an interrogative sentence. An *interrogative sentence* is one that asks a question. A question mark can be used after a word or sentence that expresses strong emotion, such as shock or doubt.

> Will the plane arrive on time?
> What? Are you serious?

A question mark can be part of a sentence that contains a quotation. Place the question mark inside the quotation marks when the quote asks a question. Place the question mark outside the quotation marks if the entire sentence asks a question.

> Teresa asked, "Will the work be finished soon?"
> Did he say, "The sale will end on Friday"?

Exclamation Points

An **exclamation point** is a punctuation mark used to express strong emotion. Exclamation points are used at the end of a sentence or after an interjection that stands alone. An exclamation point can be used at the end of a question rather than a question mark, if the writer wishes to show strong emotion.

> Ouch! Stop hurting me!

---

6   Soft Skills for the Workplace

SUMMARY

- **(LO 1-1) Explain how hard and soft skills play a role in professionalism.**
  Someone who shows professionalism has the skills to perform specific job tasks and works well with others. A skill is something an individual does well and may be classified as a hard skill or a soft skill. Hard skills are acquired through work, education, training, or a combination of these experiences. Soft skills are the basic skills common to any job, such as reading, writing, and listening.
- **(LO 1-2) Define positive attitude.**
  Attitude is how personal thoughts or feelings affect a person's outward behavior. Individuals with a positive attitude are optimistic and look at the upside of a situation rather than the downside. Optimism enables them to look at the big picture, identify what can be changed and not be changed, and make good decisions. Positive people are enthusiastic and show interest in their jobs and activities in which they participate.
- **(LO 1-3) Discuss the importance of a professional image.**
  An image is the perception others have of a person. First impressions are usually lasting impressions. A professional image is the image an individual projects in the professional world. A professional image can have an impact on a person's ability to get a job, earn promotions, and stay employed.

GLOSSARY TERMS

Visit the G-W Learning companion website at www.g-wlearning.com/careereducation/ to review the following glossary terms.

attitude	professional image
emotional intelligence quotient (EQ)	professional network
empathy	professionalism
employability skills	resilience
hard skills	skill
image	soft skills
networking	

REVIEW

1. Define professionalism.

2. Explain how hard and soft skills play a role in professionalism.

3. Explain emotional intelligence quotient (EQ).

4. Define positive attitude and resilience.

Copyright Goodheart-Willcox Co., Inc.

Professionalism

Uber Images/Shutterstock.com

BEFORE YOU READ

Before you begin reading this chapter, see what you already know about soft skills by taking a pretest. The soft skills pretest is available at **www.g-wlearning.com/careereducation/**

LEARNING OUTCOMES

On completion of this chapter, prepare to:

1-1   Explain how hard and soft skills play a role in professionalism.

1-2   Define positive attitude.

1-3   Discuss the importance of a professional image.

Professionalism extends to every job, career, and industry.

wavebreakmedia/Shutterstock.com

Skills of a Professional

Professionalism is the act of exhibiting appropriate character, judgment, and behavior by a person who is trained to perform a job. It is a person's conduct while at work or representing an employer. Professionalism extends to every job, career, and industry. It doesn't necessarily mean wearing a suit, but instead conducting oneself in a manner that exhibits responsibility, integrity, and excellence.

A professional employee comes to work on time each day and performs job tasks in a productive manner. Professionals dress appropriately for their job, take responsibility for their behavior, and are good communicators. They also possess qualities of integrity, honesty, and a positive attitude.

Someone who shows professionalism has the skills to perform specific job tasks and works well with others. A **skill** is something an individual does well. Skills can be categorized as hard skills or soft skills.

Hard Skills

Hard skills are critical skills necessary to perform the required work-related tasks of a position. They are teachable, clearly defined, and can be measured. Examples of hard skills, also called *job-specific skills*, include the ability to perform accounting tasks, repair a computer, and change the brakes on a car. Additional examples are shown in Figure 1-1.

Hard skills are acquired through work, education, training, or a combination of these experiences. The basic hard skills needed for a specific job are generally standard from business to business. For example, the hard skills required for an accounting clerk position would be very similar or the same at several different companies. Without possessing the required hard skills, an individual is unlikely to successfully perform a given job.

When applying for a job, an interviewer will ask the candidate to identify and describe the hard skills that he or she possesses. The candidate may be required to demonstrate some of those skills as part of the interview process. For example, if applying for a job as an order processor, a keyboarding test may be part of the application process. The applicant's *hard skills* are compared to the requirements for the job to see if that person meets the standards. Once a job is earned, acquiring new hard skills can be a way to earn promotions.

Figure 1-1 Hard skills are critical skills necessary to perform the required work-related tasks of a position.

Examples of Hard Skills

- accounting
- automotive repair
- barbering
- business management
- carpentry
- commercial driving
- computer programming
- data mining
- editing
- electrical engineering
- graphic designing
- keyboarding
- manufacturing plant operations
- marketing
- network security
- nursing
- pipefitting
- speaking a foreign language
- tax preparation
- welding

Goodheart-Willcox Publisher

Soft Skills

You may be the most highly-qualified person in your field in terms of hard skills, but if you lack soft skills, it may be challenging to become or stay employed. **Soft skills** are the skills used to communicate and work well with others. They are considered essential **employability skills**, which are skills that help an individual find a job, perform well in the workplace, and gain success in a job or career. Some soft skills are gained through life experience and social interaction. Other soft skills may be acquired from working at a job and interacting in professional situations. They are not specific to one career and are transferable to any type of position. Examples of desirable soft skills are shown in Figure 1-2.

When applying for employment, a job description may refer to soft skills as *people skills* or *interpersonal skills*. Employers look for well-rounded employees who have the hard skills to perform in the job and the people skills to get along with coworkers, managers, and customers.

Soft skills come easier to some people than others. The people who find soft skills easy to acquire often have a high emotional intelligence quotient. A person's **emotional intelligence quotient (EQ)** is the ability of a person to perceive emotions in one's self and in others and use this information to guide social behavior. Many soft skills rely on a person's ability to communicate with and anticipate the needs of others, as well as to meet those needs appropriately. Therefore, someone with a high EQ is often adept with soft skills.

People who have a high EQ are able to understand emotions in other people easily and react accordingly. These individuals are seen as pleasant and empathetic. Having **empathy** means having the ability to share someone else's emotions. This often results in better social interactions and relationships, including those with family, friends, coworkers, and supervisors.

Individuals with a high EQ also tend to have a better self-image, which contributes to increased self-confidence and positivity. This can have a beneficial impact on a person's working life, which leads to higher work performance and better social interactions in the workplace. Overall, those with a high EQ tend to experience a higher sense of satisfaction in life and have lower incidences of feeling insecure or depressed.

Figure 1-2 Soft skills are the skills used to communicate and work well with others.

Examples of Soft Skills

- active listening
- adaptability
- assertiveness
- collaboration
- conflict resolution
- courtesy
- critical thinking
- digital citizenship
- effective communication
- emotional control

- ethical decision making
- goal setting
- leadership
- negotiating
- patience
- positive attitude
- problem solving
- professional image
- reading
- reliability

- respectfulness
- self-confidence
- self-motivation
- thinking on your feet
- time management
- trustworthiness
- work independently
- writing

Goodheart-Willcox Publisher

Positive Attitude

Professionals exhibit a positive attitude in their job performance and workplace interactions. **Attitude** is how personal thoughts or feelings affect a person's outward behavior. It is a combination of how you feel, what you think, and what you do. Attitude is how an individual sees himself or herself, as well as how he or she perceives others.

Individuals with a *positive attitude* are optimistic and look at the upside of a situation rather than the downside. Optimism enables them to look at the big picture, identify what can be changed, recognize what cannot be changed, and make good decisions. Optimists learn from experiences, accurately identify problems, and try to offer solutions, rather than complaints. Optimistic people are proactive and learn from their mistakes.

Attitude influences the way a person performs in a job situation. People with a positive attitude generally are successful in their work life. Positive people are enthusiastic and show interest in their jobs and the activities in which they participate.

Case Study

Helga Esteb/Shutterstock.com

Professional Image

Journalist Brian Williams had a well-crafted, professional image. His image projected honesty, integrity, and the ability to communicate complex stories and issues in a way that was understandable and engaging for the common person. His image also projected likability during broadcasts, as well as in appearances outside of the news industry. In early 2015, his professional image came into conflict with the facts of a story he had reported in 2003. The story involved a military helicopter he was a passenger in during the 2003 invasion of Iraq. After the initial report, Williams retold the story many times, but the retellings included differing accounts of what happened. In a January 2015 news broadcast, he reported that his helicopter had been hit by enemy fire and was forced down. This version of events was quickly criticized by a flight engineer on another helicopter involved in the incident. Williams' reporting came under scrutiny, including many past stories. Ultimately, Williams was suspended for six months by NBC and he lost the network's nightly news anchor position.

1. What is your opinion in how image played a role in Williams presenting differing accounts of what happened?

2. Discuss how this event affected the audience's perceived honesty and integrity of Williams.

3. How should Williams have handled the situation after the first erroneous retelling of the story?

4. Describe the professional image of Brian Williams today now that the incident has lost some of its public attention.

They are eager to learn new tasks and make an effort to have productive relationships with those around them.

People who have positive attitudes are generally more resilient. **Resilience** is a person's ability to cope with and recover from change or adversity. Resilient people are able to aptly handle challenges in one aspect of their lives while not letting it affect other aspects. They can bounce back even when they feel as if they have been knocked down.

You can learn to develop a positive attitude and resilience by looking at the good things rather than dwelling on the bad. Realize that there are things that you can change to improve a situation and some things you cannot change. Learn to work with or around the things that cannot be changed. Understand that you are not personally responsible for everything that happens around you. You can choose to have a positive outlook or negative outlook on your life.

Image of a Professional

An **image** is the perception others have of a person based on that person's dress, behavior, and speech. It is what people remember about a person from business, professional, and even social interactions. A **professional image** is the image an individual projects in the professional world. A positive professional image projects honesty, skill, courtesy, and respect for others.

First impressions are usually lasting impressions. Those with whom you come in contact will most likely begin forming an opinion of you immediately, whether or not they realize it. They may not know about your education or other credentials, but the image you project can influence whether you are a person with whom they want to become acquainted.

Image begins with the way you look, but it goes well beyond what a person can see. Your behavior is equally important. Professionals have a positive attitude and a friendly disposition. They avoid gossip, negative comments about their employers and coworkers, and inappropriate subject matter when engaged in conversation with others.

Professionals exhibit confidence through body language and good manners. Initiating an introduction and handshake is a sure sign of an individual who understands the importance of soft skills. Good communication skills, especially listening, are valuable in any business or social situation.

Networking is also an important element of a person's professional image. **Networking** means talking with people you know and developing new relationships that can lead to potential career or job opportunities. A **professional network** is a group of professionals you know and who know you. These people are supportive in your career endeavors and may or may not be social friends. *LinkedIn* is an example of a professional networking site that should be used for professional purposes and not a popularity forum. Often, you are judged by the company you keep. Be conscious of those in your professional network. They can be an important part of your professional image.

A professional image can have an impact on a person's ability to get a job, earn promotions, and stay employed. Your career opportunities can be enhanced or hindered by how you demonstrate professionalism.

LinkedIn is an example of a professional networking site.

Evan Lorne/Shutterstock.com

SUMMARY

- **(LO 1-1) Explain how hard and soft skills play a role in professionalism.**
  Someone who shows professionalism has the skills to perform specific job tasks and works well with others. A skill is something an individual does well and may be classified as a hard skill or a soft skill. Hard skills are acquired through work, education, training, or a combination of these experiences. Soft skills are the basic skills common to any job, such as reading, writing, and listening.

- **(LO 1-2) Define positive attitude.**
  Attitude is how personal thoughts or feelings affect a person's outward behavior. Individuals with a positive attitude are optimistic and look at the upside of a situation rather than the downside. Optimism enables them to look at the big picture, identify what can be changed and not be changed, and make good decisions. Positive people are enthusiastic and show interest in their jobs and activities in which they participate.

- **(LO 1-3) Discuss the importance of a professional image.**
  An image is the perception others have of a person. First impressions are usually lasting impressions. A professional image is the image an individual projects in the professional world. A professional image can have an impact on a person's ability to get a job, earn promotions, and stay employed.

GLOSSARY TERMS

Visit the G-W Learning companion website at **www.g-wlearning.com/careereducation/** to review the following glossary terms.

attitude	professional image
emotional intelligence quotient (EQ)	professionalism
empathy	professional network
employability skills	resilience
hard skills	skill
image	soft skills
networking	

REVIEW

1. Define professionalism.

2. Explain how hard and soft skills play a role in professionalism.

3. Explain emotional intelligence quotient (EQ).

4. Define positive attitude and resilience.

5. Describe networking and its role in a professional image.

APPLICATION

1. Recall a situation in which you observed a person in a business situation who exhibited unprofessional behavior. State the instance and the person's behavior. How did the situation conclude or resolve?

2. Create a list of your hard skills (job-specific skills). Describe each skill, and rate your level of competency. Spend time developing this list so that you may include these skills on your résumé.

3. Create a list of the soft skills (employability skills) you have developed over the years. Why is it important for you to identify your employability skills?

4. Describe your personal emotional intelligence quotient (EQ).

5. *Empathy* is the ability to share someone else's emotions. *Sympathy* is feeling sorry for someone's unfortunate situation. There is a fine line between empathy and sympathy. People may want someone to share their emotions, but not feel sorry for them. Describe how you would coach a coworker to distinguish between empathy and sympathy.

6. Evaluate your attitude, in general, and how it has helped or hindered your personal or professional life.

7. Write a paragraph describing how you think peers would summarize your attitude.

8. How would you describe your personal level of resiliency? Cite examples of situations in which you were resilient and how you handled each.

9. Describe your professional image. How would others perceive you based on your dress, behavior, and speech?

10. If you use LinkedIn, review your contacts and update or edit the list. If you do not use LinkedIn, make a list of the primary people in your professional network. Explain the importance of your network for your professional image.

INTERNET ACTIVITY

Emotional Intelligence. Emotional intelligence quotient (EQ) is important in career success. Conduct an Internet search for an emotional intelligence quotient (EQ) assessment tool. Evaluate your personal EQ.

SKILLS PRACTICE

Visit the G-W Learning companion website at **www.g-wlearning.com/careereducation/** to access and complete the following soft skills practice activities:

Activity SS1-1 Hard Skills. Taking an inventory of your hard skills is a helpful exercise to determine your qualifications for employment. Open the SS1-1 file, and list your hard skills as directed in the document.

Activity SS1-2 Soft Skills. Assessing your soft skills will help you determine your strengths and weaknesses. Open the SS1-2 file, and complete the activity to evaluate your soft skills.

CHAPTER
2
Ethics

Idutko/Shutterstock.com

BEFORE YOU READ

Visit the G-W Learning companion website to view a video about soft skills. The video is available at **www.g-wlearning.com/careereducation/**

LEARNING OUTCOMES

On completion of this chapter, prepare to:

2-1 Define ethics.

2-2 Explain ethical communication.

2-3 Discuss the importance of digital citizenship.

A trade secret is information a company needs to keep private and protect from competitors.

PhotoSky/Shutterstock.com

Ethics

Professionals are expected to make good decisions for the business and to act ethically while on the job. **Ethics** are the moral principles or beliefs that direct a person's behavior. **Morals** are an individual's ideas of what is right and wrong. A person's sense of ethics and morals illustrates his or her integrity. *Integrity* is the honesty of a person's actions.

Ethics help people make good decisions in both their personal and professional lives. Ethical actions are those that apply ethics and moral behavior. Unethical actions are those that involve immoral behavior or crime. Criminal actions can be punishable by law.

Work ethic is the principle that honest work is its own reward. A person who has a strong work ethic believes that hard work is valuable to his or her character. Examples of behavior that demonstrate a good work ethic include arriving on time and performing duties at the highest level of ability and expectation.

Workplace ethics are principles that help define appropriate behavior in a business setting. Workplace ethics start with attendance. Ethical behavior includes arriving on time, or even early, to work each workday and putting in a full day's effort. If your day starts at 8:00 a.m., that is the time you should be at your station working. Pulling into the parking lot at 7:59 a.m. does not constitute being to work on time. Likewise, simply being in the building at 8:00 a.m. does not mean you are on time. You should be *working* at 8:00 a.m. If your day ends at 4:00 p.m., you are expected to be working until that time. Breaks and lunch breaks are not to be abused. Respect your employer's time, and conduct personal business when you are off the clock. If you need a personal day off for shopping or other reasons, make the ethical decision. Ask for a vacation day or personal day rather than pretending to be ill and requesting a sick day. These are behaviors that help an individual keep a job and potentially earn promotions. They are also examples of behaviors that reflect a person's work ethic.

Many businesses have a code of ethics that employees are expected to follow. A **code of ethics** is a document that dictates how business should be conducted. The goal of a code of ethics is to establish a value system for the company that will enable employees to make sound ethical decisions. For example, some businesses do not allow their employees to accept gifts from clients.

Some companies also establish a code of conduct. A *code of conduct* identifies the manner in which employees should behave while at work or when representing the company. The code of conduct provides guidelines of acceptable behavior in the workplace. In many instances, it functions as a set of rules to be followed with clear expectations of right and wrong actions. It can be used by a business to monitor employee behavior and discourage unacceptable behavior in the workplace. Rules that may be part of a code of conduct include the following:

- Consuming, selling, possessing, or being under the influence of alcohol or drugs during work hours or while on company property is strictly prohibited.

- Possession of firearms or other weapons on company property, during company events, or while conducting company business is strictly prohibited.

- Internet access provided by the company should be used only for business purposes, not for checking personal e-mail or shopping online.

Workplace bullying is a serious example of conduct that is unacceptable in the workplace. **Workplace bullying** is intentional, repeated mistreatment of a person by another person using verbal abuse, threats, or any other action that prevents a person from doing his or her job without fear. Such behavior can escalate to a point that it endangers an individual's well-being and can instill fear of bodily harm.

Even if not formally established by their company, professionals maintain a personal code of ethical conduct. They refrain from saying negative things about their jobs, employers, and coworkers. When they give their word to complete a task, they honor it. You can build your professional image by showing accountability for your actions and doing what you say you will do.

Ethical Communication

It is every employee's responsibility to maintain ethical behavior in all communication that represents his or her employer. *Ethical communication* is the practice of applying ethics to messages in order to ensure all communication is honest in every way.

Many companies have a communication plan in place that identifies how to ethically communicate information about the business to the public. A communication plan provides an outline of the appropriate channels of communication for the company. It also includes an analysis of how communication for the company should occur. When creating messages that represent your organization, ask the following questions to analyze if the information is ethical:

- Has confidentiality been honored?
- Has the privacy of the company been protected?
- Is the information presented factually and honestly?
- Has appropriate credit been given to contributors of the communication?
- Has copyrighted material been used appropriately?

Careful consideration must be given to the impact of company communication on the public. The point of view presented should be honest. It may be tempting for those writing messages or representing the business to get caught up in exaggerations or inaccurate claims about the company. However, doing so is unethical and may be illegal. Marketing messages that persuade the reader to buy or respond in some way must be written according to appropriate business and communication laws. These laws are enforced by the Federal Trade Commission (FTC) and dictate that truth in advertising must be followed. *False advertising* is overstating the features and benefits of products or services or making false claims about them. Misrepresenting information, intentionally or unintentionally, can lead to lawsuits, loss of customers, and loss of jobs.

It is important to choose words carefully when making comments about others, whether in person or online. **Slander** is speaking a false statement about someone that causes others to have a bad opinion of him or her. **Libel** is publishing a false statement about someone that causes others to have a bad or untrue opinion of him or her. Slander and libel can be considered crimes of defamation.

Confidentiality

Confidentiality means that specific information is never shared, except with those who have clearance to receive it. This includes information about customers and other employees. Just because a person works with you does not mean that person is entitled to confidential company information.

Proprietary information is anything that is owned by a business. It usually refers to information, products, or processes created by a company's employees on company time. Proprietary information can include many things, such as product formulas, customer lists, manufacturing processes, or other trade secrets. A *trade secret* is information a company needs to keep private and protect from competitors.

Before providing information to someone, confirm that it will not violate confidentiality. These questions can help determine if the information can be shared:

- Has confidentiality been honored?
- Has privacy of the company been protected?
- Is this a person who has been given authority to receive this information?

Professionalism should be the number one priority when representing an employer. Employees who share proprietary information with outsiders or other employees are behaving unethically and, possibly, breaking the law.

Social Responsibility

Social responsibility is behaving with sensitivity to social, environmental, and economic issues. As a professional, social responsibility may be considered an ethical issue. Negative communication about or actions toward society or the environment reflects negatively on the company. Messages and actions should be analyzed to confirm they are not offensive. Consider the following questions when evaluating the social responsibility of actions or communications:

- Have any negative comments been stated or implied about social issues, such as the environment?
- Have any personal opinions about social responsibility been included?

Digital Citizenship

It is important to understand the difference between ethical and unethical activities related to technology and online conduct, especially in the workplace. **Digital citizenship** is the standard of appropriate behavior when using technology. Good digital citizenship focuses on using technology in a positive manner, rather than using it for negative or illegal purposes. Our daily lives revolve around using technology in many shapes and forms. However, people who participate in the digital society have a legal responsibility for their online actions, whether those actions are ethical or unethical. It is necessary to learn to communicate ethically and appropriately within a digital society.

Information posted on the Internet never really goes away. A *digital footprint* is a data record of all an individual's online activities. Even if you delete something you have posted on the Internet, it is still stored in your digital footprint. Always think before posting to social media sites or sending an e-mail. What you post online today could risk your future career opportunities.

Etiquette is the art of using good manners in any situation. Digital etiquette, or *netiquette*, is etiquette used when communicating electronically and interacting on the Internet. It includes accepted social and professional guidelines for Internet-based communication. These guidelines apply to e-mail, social media, and other contact with customers and peers via the Internet. For example, using all capital letters in a message is not acceptable because it implies the writer is yelling. Proper capitalization, spelling, and grammar should always be used.

Cyberbullying is using electronic technology to harass or threaten an individual. It includes using social media, text messages, or e-mails to harass or scare a person with hurtful words or pictures. The victim of cyberbullying is often not physically seen or touched by a bully. However, this does not mean the person cannot be harmed by the bully's actions. Cyberbullying is not only unethical, in many cases it can be prosecuted as a criminal act. Flaming and spamming are unethical actions that violate netiquette and, depending on the severity, can be considered cyberbullying. *Flaming* is purposefully insulting someone and inciting an argument on social media. *Spamming* is sending unwanted mass e-mails or intentionally flooding an individual's social media site or e-mail inbox with unwanted messages.

An important aspect of digital citizenship is respecting an employer's property and time. Internet access provided by the company should be used only for business purposes. For example, checking personal e-mail or playing a game online is not acceptable. Most companies have an established acceptable use policy. An *acceptable use policy* is a set of rules that explains what is and is not acceptable use of company-owned and company-operated equipment and networks. Employees are typically made aware of acceptable use policies during training before they are allowed access to the company's computers and network.

Case Study

s_bukley/Shutterstock.com

Social Responsibility

While working with the United Nations World Food Programme, Lauren Bush witnessed the devastating effects of hunger firsthand and decided she wanted to do more for world hunger. Bush, who had studied fashion design, began creating simple, reusable tote bags. She intended that the proceeds from the sales of these bags to go directly to World Food Programme. However, many legal and logistical problems working with the United Nations nearly doomed the program. Undeterred, Bush decided to start her own company called FEED Projects to sell the bags. Each FEED bag is stamped with a number indicating how many meals or micronutrient packets have been provided by its purchase. FEED Projects funds anti-hunger programs across the world, including a partnership with Feed America. To date, FEED Projects has provided more than 94 million meals to those without food. Bush also cofounded the FEED Foundation, a nonprofit organization to raise awareness and funds to support both national and global organizations combating hunger and malnutrition.

1. What does the formation of FEED Projects suggest about Lauren Bush's sense of social responsibility?

2. What soft skills do you think Lauren used to get her initiative off the ground?

3. What hard skills do you think Lauren used to launch FEED Projects?

4. How do Lauren Bush's actions affect her professional image?

Intellectual Property

The Internet provides countless sources for obtaining text, images, video, audio, and software. Even though this material is easily obtainable, it may not be available for you to use in any way you choose. Laws exist to govern the use of media and creative works. The creators or owners of material posted on the Internet have certain legal rights. **Intellectual property** is something that comes from a person's mind, such as an idea, invention, or process. Intellectual property laws protect a person's or company's inventions, artistic works, and other intellectual property.

Plagiarism is claiming another person's material as one's own, which is both unethical and illegal. If you must refer to someone else's work, follow intellectual property laws to acquire the information ethically. Use standard methods of citing sources. Citation guidelines in references such as *The Chicago Manual of Style* and the Modern Language Association's *MLA Handbook* can be helpful.

Piracy is the unethical and illegal copying or downloading of software, files, and other protected material. Examples of protected material include images, movies, and music. Piracy carries a heavy penalty, including fines and incarceration.

Copyrights

A *copyright* acknowledges ownership of a work and specifies that only the owner has the right to sell the work, use it, or give permission for someone else to sell or use it. Any use of copyrighted material without permission is called *infringement*. Copyright laws cover all original work, whether it is in print, on the Internet, or in any other media format. Scanning a document does not make the content yours.

Copyrighted material is indicated by the © symbol or the statement "copyright by." Material that does not include the symbol or statement may still be copyrighted. All original material is automatically copyrighted as soon as it is in a tangible form. An idea cannot be copyrighted. A copyright can be registered with the US Copyright Office, which is part of the Library of Congress. However, original material is still legally protected whether or not the copyright is registered.

Most information on the Internet is copyrighted, whether it is text, graphics, illustrations, or digital media. This means it cannot be reused without obtaining permission from the owner. Sometimes, the owner of the material places it on the Internet specifically for others to reuse. However, if this is not explicitly stated, assume the material is copyrighted and cannot be freely used.

Many websites list rules for use of content, called the *terms of use*, which must be followed for downloaded files. The terms of use agreement may come up automatically, for example, if you are downloading a file or software application. If, however, you are copying an image or a portion of text from a website, you will need to look for the terms of use information. Unless the terms of use specifically state that you are free to copy and use the material provided on a website, assume the material is copyrighted. You cannot reuse the material without permission.

Photocopying copyrighted material without permission is called infringement.

lightpoet/Shutterstock.com

Fair use doctrine allows individuals to use copyrighted works without permission in limited situations under very strict guidelines. Fair use doctrine allows copyrighted material to be used for the purpose of describing or reviewing the work. For example, a student writing about copyrighted material in an original report is an example of fair use. Another example is a product-review website that provides editorial comment. Fair use doctrine does not change the copyright or ownership of the material used under the doctrine.

In some cases, individuals or organizations may wish to allow others to use their intellectual property without requiring permission. This type of use assignment may be called *copyleft*, which is a play on the word *copyright*. One popular method of allowing use of intellectual property is a Creative Commons license. A *Creative Commons (CC) license* is a specialized copyright license that allows free distribution of copyrighted work. If the creator of the work wants to give the public the ability to use, share, or advance his or her original work, a Creative Commons license provides that flexibility. The creator maintains the copyright and can specify how the copyrighted work can be used.

Public domain refers to material that is not owned by anybody and can be used without permission. Material can enter the public domain when a copyright expires and is not renewed. Much of the material created by federal, state, and local governments is often in the public domain. This is because taxpayer money was used to create it. Additionally, the owner of the material may choose to give up ownership and place the material in the public domain.

A *licensing agreement* is a contract that gives one party permission to market, produce, or use the good or service owned by another party. The agreement grants a license in return for a fee or royalty payment. When buying software, the purchaser agrees to follow the terms of a license. A *license* is the legal permission to use a software program. All software has terms of use that explain how and when the software may be used. Figure 2-1 explains the characteristics of different software licensing.

Alternative usage rights for software programs are typically covered by the *GNU General Public License (GNU GPL)*. The GNU GPL guarantees all users the freedom to use, study, share, and modify the software. The term *open source* applies to software that has had its source code made available to the public at no charge. Open-source software can be downloaded and used for free and can be modified and distributed by anyone. However, part or all of the code of open-source software may be owned by an individual or organization.

Figure 2-1 The terms of use outlined in a software license vary depending on the type of software.

Software Licenses		
Software Type	**Cost**	**Features**
For-Purchase	Must be purchased to use; demo version may be available	Full functionality
Freeware	Never have to pay for use	Full functionality
Shareware	Free to try; must pay for upgrade to full functionality	Limited functionality without upgrade

Goodheart-Willcox Publisher

SUMMARY

- **(LO 2-1) Define ethics.**
  Ethics are the moral principles or beliefs that direct a person's behavior. A code of ethics is a document that dictates how business should be conducted, while a code of conduct identifies the manner in which employees should behave while at work or when representing the company.

- **(LO 2-2) Explain ethical communication.**
  Ethical communication is the practice of applying ethics to messages in order to ensure all communication is honest in every way. Confidentiality means that specific communication is never shared, except with those who have clearance to receive it. Social responsibility is behaving with sensitivity to social, environmental, and economic issues. Negative communication about or actions toward society or the environment reflects negatively on the company.

- **(LO 2-3) Discuss the importance of digital citizenship.**
  Digital citizenship is the standard of appropriate behavior when using technology. People who participate in the digital society have a legal responsibility for their online actions, whether those actions are ethical or unethical. Technology should be used in a positive manner rather than using it for negative or illegal purposes. This behavior also applies to intellectual property and copyrights.

GLOSSARY TERMS

Visit the G-W Learning companion website at **www.g-wlearning.com/careereducation/** to review the following glossary terms.

code of ethics	morals
confidentiality	piracy
cyberbullying	plagiarism
digital citizenship	proprietary information
ethics	slander
etiquette	social responsibility
intellectual property	work ethic
libel	workplace bullying

REVIEW

1. Define ethics.

2. What is the potential outcome of unethical communication for a company or business?

3. List examples of guidelines that should be used to determine if confidential material should be shared with another person.

4. List two questions that can be used to determine if a message or action is offensive.

5. Discuss the importance of digital citizenship.

APPLICATION

1. How does a person develop morals and ethics? Cite examples of situations in which a person's morals and ethics changed over time and events that influenced the change.

2. Write a paragraph that describes your personal ethics.

3. Write a paragraph that highlights your own work ethics.

4. Peer pressure can be strong in an employment situation. Behavior of coworkers that is in conflict with the company code of conduct should not be used as an excuse for others to deviate in their behavior. Cite examples of negative behavior by a coworker that, if you followed, might result in you losing your job.

5. Assume that you have created and documented a process that streamlines the company's production. If you were to accept a job at a different company, should you be able to take a copy of that document to the new job? Why or why not?

6. Most people think they are socially responsible. Describe your personal level of social responsibility.

7. You have been invited to speak to members of your team about the importance of digital citizenship for the workplace. Outline the specific topics you would discuss. How can you make the connection that each of these topics has an ethical implication?

8. Your digital footprint is important to your personal life as well as your future professional career. List examples of activities that may have a negative impact on your career if you posted about them on a social media website.

9. Intellectual property is something that comes from a person's mind. Ideas, however, cannot be copyrighted until they are in tangible form. Explain how you would handle a situation in which you have an idea for a good or service that a coworker claims was his or her idea.

10. A license is a specific copyright that grants a user permission to use a software program. If you buy software that states you can install the software on as many of your personal computers as you choose, is it okay to also install it on a friend's computer? Why or why not?

INTERNET ACTIVITY

Workplace Bullying. Workplace bullying is an increasingly growing problem for workers and employers. Conduct an Internet search for workplace bullying. After you have reviewed several articles, describe how you would coach a coworker to identify if he or she is being bullied. Next, outline steps you would suggest taking to approach the employer on the issue and how to resolve it.

Social Media Postings. Employees can be fired for posting inappropriate information on social media. A post, such as "I hate my boss," can cost an individual his or her job. Conduct a search for people who were fired for publishing negative material that their employers discovered.

SKILLS PRACTICE

Visit the G-W Learning companion website at **www.g-wlearning.com/careereducation/** to access and complete the following soft skills practice activities:

Activity SS2-1 Confidentiality. Confidentiality is an ethical and legal issue for organizations. Open the SS2-1 file, and read a customer confidentiality policy as stated by a business. Discuss why that violation of customer confidentiality could be a legal issue for an organization.

Activity SS2-2 Ethics Checklist. Ethical behavior is important in both personal and professional lives. An ethics checklist can help analyze difficult situations. Open the SS2-2 file, and create an ethics checklist. Then, using that checklist, analyze the situations that follow.

CHAPTER 3

Self-Management Skills

Elnur/Shutterstock.com

BEFORE YOU READ

Visit the G-W Learning companion website to view a video about soft skills. The video is available at **www.g-wlearning.com/careereducation/**

LEARNING OUTCOMES

On completion of this chapter, prepare to:

3-1   Cite examples of self-management skills.

3-2   Define stress-management skills.

The lack of emotional control in a workplace situation can cost an individual his or her job.

michaelhelm/Shutterstock.com

Developing Self-Management Skills

Self-management skills are the skills that enable an individual to control and make the best use of his or her time and abilities. These are important soft skills that should be developed to the highest-possible level. They are important because they facilitate productivity, help ensure employee success, and provide assurance for an employer that the employee will help the business meet its goals. An individual has complete control over the development and use of self-management skills. These are skills that positive people strive to develop. Some important self-management skills are emotional control, problem solving, time management, and goal setting. There are many others that you probably can think of to add to this list.

Emotional Control

Learning how to manage emotions helps a person think logically and act appropriately. **Emotional control** is the process of directing one's feelings and reactions toward a desirable result that is socially acceptable. The lack of emotional control in a workplace situation can cost an individual his or her job.

As you recall, a person's *Emotional Intelligence Quotient (EQ)* is the ability of a person to perceive emotions in one's self and use this information to guide his or her social behavior. People with a high EQ are probably more adept at emotional control.

Most people experience negative emotions at work from time to time. *Negativity* is a state in which a person cannot acknowledge positive qualities. Frustration, disappointment, and challenging situations are as much a part of work as they are of everyday life. For example, a colleague might be demanding, or a customer might be rude. When you experience a negative emotion at work, take a minute to pause and evaluate the situation. Try to understand the cause of your feelings and what you can do to help the situation. Adding more negativity to a situation usually only makes matters worse. Look for an action that is helpful, not hurtful. Focusing on the positive in an emotional situation can help you maintain control over your personal feelings.

Criticism is a common source of negative emotions at work. *Criticism* is a comment that expresses unfavorable judgment or disapproval of a person or action. **Constructive criticism** is criticism offered in a friendly manner with the objective of improving outcome and performance of another person. It is often given as a form of advice, not as an act of disrespect.

It is inevitable that when on the job, you will receive constructive criticism from your employer and/or coworkers. When criticism is given and accepted in a professional manner, it can help an individual grow and improve chances of success in a career. When someone offers you constructive criticism,

- listen and resist the temptation to become angry or defensive;
- ask questions and make sure you understand the feedback that is being offered; and
- work to address the input that you received.

A first response to criticism might be to become angry or defensive. However, exercising emotional control is important, as well as remembering that the words are not intended to diminish your self-esteem.

Problem Solving

Problem solving is a process of choosing a course of action after evaluating available information and weighing the costs, benefits, and consequences of alternative actions.

It involves critical thinking and the ability to use prior knowledge, data, and good judgment to solve problems.

Most of what an individual does each day involves solving problems. It can be as simple as deciding where to go to lunch or as complicated as brainstorming what to do about the company's declining sales. Employers value employees who are problem solvers, not complainers. Every business relies on its employees to demonstrate how to solve problems that arise each day. Applying systematic problem solving as a self-management skill is a necessary job skill. There are five general steps to this process, as illustrated in Figure 3-1.

1. *Define the problem.* A clear idea of the problem must be formulated in order to find the best approach.

2. *Explore all alternatives.* Potential solutions to the challenge should be listed and analyzed.

3. *Choose the best alternative.* After considering all potential solutions, the one that best fits the situation can be selected. It may be a single alternative or some combination of alternatives.

4. *Act on the decision.* Once a decision is made, it should be executed.

5. *Evaluate the solution or decision.* After time has passed, the solution can be analyzed to determine if it was the correct course of action.

Problem solving involves critical-thinking skills. **Critical-thinking skills** are skills that provide the ability to analyze and interpret a situation and make reasonable judgments and decisions. When you apply critical-thinking skills, you try to eliminate emotions and be open-minded about the possibilities. Then, a solution or process can be applied so that a productive action can be taken. Applying critical-thinking skills can help solve problems in a more efficient manner.

Time Management

Time management is the practice of organizing time and work assignments to increase personal efficiency. Tasks must be prioritized by determining which ones should be completed before others. The difference between average and excellent workers is often not how hard they work, but how well they prioritize tasks. Creating a list of tasks to do each day is one simple way to manage your time. For example, you *have* to attend a business meeting. You *do not have* to check social media sites while you are working, so it should not be on your list of tasks for the day. It is also important to schedule lunch and breaks. Leaving your desk, even for just a few minutes, can help you relax and avoid feeling trapped at your job.

Figure 3-1 Problem solving is a process of choosing a course of action after evaluating available information and weighing the costs, benefits, and consequences of alternative actions.

Goodheart-Willcox Publisher

Interruptions and unplanned events are inevitable and may occur during the workday. Time management requires that an individual balance unscheduled coworker visits and other tasks that demand attention. If you have an especially busy day of tasks that need attention, post a "do not disturb" sign on your door.

Personal information management (PIM) is a system that individuals use to acquire, organize, maintain, retrieve, and use information. An example of a PIM system is Microsoft Outlook. This software can be used to create a schedule, record contact information, and complete other activities that help organize personal information. It is also an e-mail client used for communication.

Goal Setting

Setting goals helps facilitate time management. A **goal** is something to be achieved in a specified time period. *Goal setting* is the process of deciding what needs to be achieved and defining the time period. There are two types of goals: short-term and long-term. A *short-term goal* is one that can be achieved in less than one year. A *long-term goal* is one that will take a longer period of time to achieve, usually more than one year.

Well-defined goals, including career goals, follow the SMART goal model. **SMART goals** are specific, measurable, attainable, realistic, and timely. Figure 3-2 illustrates the five elements of a SMART goal.

Specific

A goal should be specific and straightforward. For example, "I want to have a career" is not specific. Instead, you might say, "I want to have a career in writing." When the goal is specific, it is easier to track your progress. It also helps in identifying tasks that need to be completed to achieve the goal.

Measurable

It is important to be able to measure progress so you know when you have reached your goal. For example, "I want to earn a master degree in journalism" is a measurable goal. When you earn the degree, you will know your goal has been reached.

Figure 3-2 SMART goals are specific, measurable, attainable, realistic, and timely.

Goodheart-Willcox Publisher

Attainable

Goals need to be attainable. For example, "I want to be editor-in-chief at a newspaper in two years after graduating" is not a reasonable goal for that point in a person's career. Gaining work experience is necessary before obtaining an executive position. The goal of being an editor-in-chief becomes more attainable when coupled with a plan to gain the necessary skills and experience.

Realistic

Goals must be realistic. Obtaining a position as editor-in-chief at a newspaper may be practical with proper planning. However, it is not realistic for an entry-level employee. Finding an entry-level position as a reporter and working your way up to editor-in-chief over a period of years is a realistic goal.

Timely

A goal should have starting and ending points. Setting a time frame to achieve a goal is the step most often overlooked. An end date can help you stay on track. For example, you may want to be editor-in-chief by the time you are 35 years old. Aiming to get the experience and education to achieve this position by a specific age will help you remain motivated to reach your goal on time.

Case Study

Kent Sievers/Shutterstock.com

Time Management

Warren Buffett is a famous investor and one of the world's wealthiest people. He is the chairman of the board, president, and CEO of Berkshire Hathaway, Inc., which is a multinational holding company. Berkshire Hathaway fully or partially owns dozens of companies, and its net worth is around $300 billion. One would think Buffett maintains a full schedule in operating Berkshire Hathaway, yet he is known for keeping his calendar almost completely clear. It is reported that one of the ways he is able to do this is through a simple three-step process of prioritizing. The first step in this process is to make a list of the 25 most important things to do. Next, circle the top five things on that list. The top five things are what you should focus on. The last step is to throw out the 20 items that you did not circle. These items are simply distractions to the five most important items.

1. Why is prioritizing an important element of time management?

2. What does having a clear calendar say about Buffett's time-management skills?

3. The last step of the three-step process of prioritizing is to discard any item that is not in the top five priorities. Explain why it is important for these additional items to be deleted.

4. How do Buffett's time-management skills contribute to his professional image?

Scheduling regular exercise is one way to relieve stress.

Dragon Images/Shutterstock.com

Stress-Management Skills

Stress-management skills are the skills that enable an individual to identify and control stress. **Stress** is the body's reaction to increased demands or dangerous situations. It can manifest itself in many ways, including nervousness, anger, feeling overwhelmed, frequent headaches, upset stomach, or even high blood pressure.

All of the responsibilities, expectations, and activities that exist in our personal and professional lives can create a great deal of anxiety and pressure. *Stress management* is a variety of strategies used to cope with stress and limit its effects. Figure 3-3 identifies some common stress-management strategies.

A certain amount of stress can be positive in the workplace. Some people are driven to perform when pressured to meet a deadline. Others react to the release of adrenaline that stress triggers, which speeds up the heart and increases metabolism for endurance. The goal is to identify the good stress as well as the negative stress in your life. When stress becomes negative, it is time to evaluate and get help if needed.

Figure 3-3 Stress-management skills are the skills that enable an individual to identify and control stress.

Stress-Management Strategies	
Identify stress triggers	• Where were you when you started feeling stressed? • What activity were you engaged in? • Was there a particular situation or conversation involved? • Were there other people around you that may have contributed to your stress?
Attend to physical needs	• Get an adequate amount of sleep • Eat regular meals • Avoid foods that provide a quick jolt of energy, such as sugar and caffeine • Schedule regular exercise
Practice time management	• Schedule tasks and meeting for the day • Plan time for breaks and lunch
Be proactive, not reactive	• Focus on the positive • Deal with the challenge rather than worry • Set realistic goals • Find balance in personal and professional life

Goodheart-Willcox Publisher

SUMMARY

- **(LO 3-1) Cite examples of self-management skills.**
  Self-management skills are the skills that enable an individual to control and direct his or her time and achievement. Examples of self-management skills are emotional control, problem solving, time management, and goal setting.
- **(LO 3-2) Define stress-management skills.**
  Stress management skills are the skills that enable an individual to identify and control stress. Stress is the body's reaction to increased demands or dangerous situations.

GLOSSARY TERMS

Visit the G-W Learning companion website at **www.g-wlearning.com/careereducation/** to review the following glossary terms.

constructive criticism	self-management skills
critical-thinking skills	SMART goals
emotional control	stress
goal	stress-management skills
personal information management (PIM)	time management
problem solving	

REVIEW

1. Describe self-management skills and cite examples.

2. Define emotional control.

3. Identify the steps for successful problem solving.

4. List the five qualities of a SMART goal.

5. Define stress-management skills.

APPLICATION

1. Identify a self-management skill in which you are proficient. Explain why you think you are proficient in that specific skill.

2. Write a paragraph describing your emotional control. Next, write a paragraph describing your emotional control from the perspective of coworkers. How are the two perspectives the same or different?

3. Reflect on a situation in which an employer or coworker offered you constructive criticism. Describe your feelings, your response, and how you applied the advice.

4. You have been presented with the issue of inadequate parking spaces for all the employees in your company. Apply the problem-solving process to propose a solution. Be prepared to discuss your approach.

5. List all the tasks you need to complete at work in a typical day. Approximate how long each task will take to complete. Next, prioritize the importance of each task. Identify any tasks that are dependent on other tasks. When you have finished your list, create a plan for managing your time for the day that will allow you to complete all the tasks.

6. Calculate the amount of time you generally spend on personal activities in a day. Include leisure time such as watching television or reading a book. Where is the majority of your time spent? Explain how you can better manage your time to be more productive in your personal life.

7. Observe a friend or colleague who demonstrates positive time-management skills. What do you think makes that person successful?

8. Identify one short-term goal that you have set for yourself. Evaluate it against the criteria for a SMART goal. Explain why your goal meets each criterion of a SMART goal or describe how you can alter the goal to make it match.

9. Identify one long-term goal that you have set for yourself. Evaluate it against the criteria for a SMART goal. Explain why your goal meets each criterion of a SMART goal or describe how you can alter the goal to make it match.

10. Reflect on the level of stress you experience during a normal workday. Identify the causes of stress and how you can cope in a positive manner.

INTERNET ACTIVITY

Emotional Control. Displaying negative emotions in the workplace can cost a person his or her job. Conduct research on loss of emotional control at work. Locate an article that describes negative behavior of an employee who suffered consequences because of lack of emotional control. Summarize the outcome for that person.

Stress-Management Skills. Learning to cope with stress is an important skill to learn for an individual's well-being. Conduct research on stress-management skills. Note ways you can identify stress in your life and apply stress-management techniques to help you cope.

SKILLS PRACTICE

Visit the G-W Learning companion website at **www.g-wlearning.com/careereducation/** to access and complete the following soft skills practice activities:

Activity SS3-1 Time-Management Skills. Time management is an important soft skill that can help a person be effective in his or her career. Complete the activity in the SS3-1 file to rate your personal time-management skills.

Activity SS3-2 Problem Solving. The first step of finding a solution is to first identify the problem. Open the SS3-2 file, and define the problem statement for each situation.

Activity SS3-3 Stress Evaluation. To effectively manage stress, sources of stress must be identified and its effects recognized. Open the SS3-3 file, and evaluate your level of stress.

CHAPTER 4

Etiquette

lightwavemedia/Shutterstock.com

BEFORE YOU READ

Visit the G-W Learning companion website to view a video about soft skills. The video is available at **www.g-wlearning.com/careereducation/**

LEARNING OUTCOMES

On completion of this chapter, prepare to:

4-1   Define professional etiquette.

4-2   Cite examples of behaviors that show respect for company workspace.

4-3   Identify guidelines for digital devices in the workplace.

4-4   Discuss proper business dining etiquette.

4-5   Summarize appropriate funeral etiquette.

Etiquette

Etiquette is the art of using good manners in any situation. *Professional etiquette* is applying the rules of good manners in the workplace and in other work-related situations.

Practicing professional etiquette can help an individual build relationships with coworkers, employers, and customers. It takes almost no effort to be mannerly, and yet the effort has big payoffs. Saying "please," "thank you," and "you're welcome" are common courtesies. Greeting coworkers with "good morning" or "how are you today" reflects positively on your professional image. Examples of professional etiquette are shown in Figure 4-1.

Protocol is a set of customs and rules that explains appropriate conduct or procedures in formal situations. *Business protocol* refers to the customs and rules found in the professional world. Many aspects of business protocol are not in written format and, therefore, must be learned from experience.

A hallmark of professionalism is respect for others. Learn the names of the people with whom you work, customers of your business with whom you interact, and those performing work for you. Address each person by name. Never judge people according to their social status or perceived importance. Treat everyone equally.

Keep your personal business personal, and refrain from asking business associates about *their* personal business. It is okay to share some information, but use good judgment concerning what you share and what you ask.

Choose words that show respect to others. Never use profane words or phrases in the workplace. To do so is inappropriate and unacceptable behavior. It is also offensive to your coworkers. Using age, gender, race, physical ability, or ethnicity as a way to describe others is unethical and sometimes illegal. Bias-free language should be the protocol for all communication, whether verbal or written, to show respect for those with whom you come in contact.

When you realize you have made a mistake, admit it and decide how to rectify the situation. Everyone makes errors, and you will gain respect by admitting your fault. It is unprofessional and unethical to blame others for your mistakes. Doing so is likely to cause others to lose confidence in your abilities and honesty.

Talking over a cubicle wall is considered rude and is a distraction to others.

Blend Images/Shutterstock.com

Figure 4-1 Professional etiquette is applying the rules of good manners in the workplace and in other work-related situations.

Examples of Professional Etiquette

- Write a thank-you note when someone does something special for you.
- Show kindness and courtesy to each person with whom you come in contact.
- Compliment those around you when they contribute in a positive manner.
- Wait to speak until it is your turn.
- Arrive on time to every meeting and appointment.
- Address each person to whom you speak by his or her name.
- Turn off your digital devices when in a meeting or conversation.
- Shake hands when meeting someone for the first time.
- Show you are listening when engaged in a conversation.
- Respect the workspaces of your coworkers.
- Do not let your actions or conversations become a disturbance in the workplace.

Goodheart-Willcox Publisher

Workspace

Business transpires in many different settings, depending on the career you have chosen. A *workplace*, or place of work, is the location where business is conducted and where employees of a company work. A *workspace* is the specific area within a company's location where an employee works. It is an individual's personal space within the workplace.

If you are a physician, for example, your workplace may be a medical office, while your workspace may be an office or exam room within the medical office. For a technician who performs equipment repair, the workplace may be a building in an industrial park, and the workspace may be a repair bay within the building or even a service van or truck.

Regardless of the type of workspace you have within your place of work, etiquette should be followed. **Workspace etiquette** is applying the rules of good manners while you are in your own workspace and the workspaces of others. Proper workspace respect helps to maintain positive relationships with coworkers, managers, and customers.

Case Study

Workplace Etiquette

Jimme48 Photography/Shutterstock.com

Serena Williams is one of the most dominant names in the world of professional tennis. She is often considered to be the greatest female tennis player of all time. However, in the 2009 US Open, her inappropriate actions cost her a semifinal match against Kim Clijsters. After losing the first set to Clijsters, Williams broke her racket by smashing it against the playing surface and net in anger. This action earned her a warning. During a tiebreak in the second set, Williams was called for a foot fault, which she argued with the lineswoman using threats and profanity. The umpire of the match intervened and awarded a point to Clijsters. That point resulted in Clijsters winning the match and advancing, while Williams was eliminated from the singles competition. By losing emotional control and ignoring the rules of etiquette, Williams cost herself a chance at advancing to the final round of the tournament.

1. The tennis court is the workspace for a tennis player. Explain how Serena's behavior toward the line judge could be considered workplace bullying.

2. When someone has a reputation as honorific as "greatest of all time," why is it important for him or her to follow rules of etiquette?

3. Describe Serena's level of emotional control during this event.

4. Professionalism is the act of exhibiting appropriate character, judgment, and behavior. How do you think the public would describe Serena's professionalism after this incident?

Respect should be shown to your employer by keeping your workspace clean, organized, and free from clutter. Over-decorating with photographs and personal items can be distracting in a business situation, so discretion should be used. Coats should be placed in the designated area rather than on the back of a chair or on top of a desk. Personal items, such as briefcases and lunch containers, should be placed in a drawer or closet to maintain discretion and safety, as well as to keep the workspace orderly.

Coworkers deserve privacy. It is polite to knock to announce your presence before entering a coworker's workspace or initiating a conversation. If delivering documents or other materials to a person who is not in his or her workspace, it is customary to place the items in a prominent place so the items will be noticed on return. This might mean placing the item in a physical inbox, on the person's chair, or on top of the computer keyboard. When placing items in an absent colleague's workspace, do not linger or look through personal items. It is inappropriate to *snoop* through someone else's property while making a delivery.

The workplace should be conducive to work, and noise can prevent others from performing their jobs. If listening to music in your workspace, use headphones. Digital devices should be turned off or put in silent mode. Always be aware of the volume of your voice, especially when talking on the phone. Use your "inside voice" as others are probably within earshot of your conversation. Talking in the hallway, outside an office, or in a cubicle can be distracting to those around you. If a conversation requires more than a few words, move the conversation into a conference room or other space where a door can be closed.

If a loud neighbor becomes a distraction and hinders your ability to work, your first response should be to have a polite conversation with the person. There is a chance the person does not realize his or her voice is too loud or that other actions have become a distraction for you. To address the issue, it is appropriate to have a face-to-face conversation rather than sending an e-mail. An e-mail can seem passive-aggressive in this situation. If you are uncomfortable speaking to the person directly, consult your supervisor or human resource manager.

Some businesses allow employees to take breaks or eat lunch at their desks. If you choose to bring food into your workspace, remember to clean up after you have finished. Dispose of any leftover food or packages in the break room instead of your workspace so as not to create odors that bother others.

Offices

Depending on your career and position, your workspace may be your own office in the workplace. Having your own office provides a quiet, private space to complete tasks. If you have an office, treat it as a privilege.

When conducting a meeting in your office, close the door. This minimizes the chance of disturbing your neighbors and discourages eavesdropping from those who pass by your door. The same is true for telephone conversations—close the door.

When visiting another person's office, knock before entering, even if the door is open. If the person is on the phone, leave and come back another time. However, if you have arrived for a planned meeting, you can motion to make sure the person sees you, and then wait in the hallway.

Cubicles

Cubicles offer some privacy, but they are not as protected from noises and other distractions as an office with a door. However, it is still the personal space of the person working there and should be treated as such. It is proper to extend the same courtesies and show the same respect as if the person's workspace were a private office.

Shared spaces, such as employee break rooms, should be kept clean and orderly.

Robert Kneschke/Shutterstock.com

When visiting a person in a cubicle, knock on the outside wall or top of the desk in the same manner you would knock on an office door. If the person is on the phone, leave and come back another time. Standing in the hallway to wait for the person to be available is inappropriate, especially if you are in an area of others working in open cubicles.

When talking to a coworker in a cubicle, walk around the walls or partitions to communicate. It is rude to raise your voice to talk over or around the wall. If you overhear others talking, try your best not to eavesdrop. Wait to be invited into a conversation rather than jumping in just because it is within earshot.

Shared Spaces

Employees are expected to keep company workspaces clean and in order, and company property should be treated with respect. When using a shared copier, remember not to leave paper clips or other supplies behind. If you remove supplies from a cabinet or closet, put them away when you are finished.

When taking breaks or eating lunch in the common eating area, clean up dishes, utensils, and food packaging. It is always better to leave an area cleaner than you found it. Food should not be removed from a refrigerator unless it is *your* food. Protocol dictates that if you pour the last cup of coffee from the community coffee pot, start brewing a new pot.

Thermostat settings in a building should not be adjusted without asking a supervisor. Many buildings have preprogrammed heating and ventilation systems that must not be tampered with. If you have issues with the temperature in your workspace, keep a sweater, space heater, or personal fan available. If the temperature is extreme and distracting to you, speak with your supervisor.

If your workplace provides a parking facility, respect what has been provided for the employees. Cars should only be parked in designated parking spots. Handicapped spaces should only be used for people who need them. A handicapped placard is *not* a parking pass. Misuse of a handicapped permit is unethical, as well as illegal, and subject to penalty.

Digital Devices

Digital devices have become a nuisance in certain workplace situations. An organization's protocol for digital devices may or may not be in writing. However, there are certain common-sense guidelines that should be followed. As a professional, it is important to display good manners and know when to refrain from digital device use.

In a meeting or other professional situation, it is unacceptable to use a digital device to check e-mail. Personal electronics should not be visible on the desk or table. A general rule is to turn them off until a meeting with coworkers or business associates has concluded. However, if it is necessary to take a phone call, excuse yourself and take the call behind closed doors. It is rude to talk on the phone when in a meeting, and coworkers do not want to hear a personal conversation.

Business Dining

There may be times when you will meet with a client or coworker for lunch to discuss business. This type of meeting may be referred to as a *dinner meeting*, although the actual meal may be breakfast, lunch, or dinner. *Business dining etiquette* is applying the rules of good manners while conducting business over a meal. This includes turning off your personal electronic devices and placing them out of sight for the duration of the meal.

You are expected to dress appropriately for a dinner meeting. Often, regardless of which meal it is conducted over, the dress for a dinner meeting is expected to be slightly more formal than would be appropriate for an in-office meeting. When in doubt, ask the person scheduling the meeting about the appropriate attire.

As with any meeting, attendees should arrive on time. Tardiness is a sign of disrespect. When you are greeted by the maître d' or waitstaff at the restaurant, indicate you are there for a meeting, and provide the name of the company or person who is hosting. Once shown to the meeting, introduce yourself to those attending the dinner. Follow the protocol for making introductions.

The highest-ranking person or the person with the most seniority should be the one to set the example. He or she should be the first to be seated and the first to order, although in many cases, this person may defer to you as a guest out of politeness. Once you are seated, the napkin should be placed on your lap. When it is your turn to order, do so quickly; this shows decisiveness. Be conservative in what you order, and avoid foods that are messy. Refrain from selecting the most expensive item or anything that requires extra prep time. It is best to err on the side of caution when ordering a beverage and choose iced tea, water, or soda water.

You will be expected to participate in conversation. Be mindful of this as you eat, and never speak with food in your mouth. Throughout the meal, be sure to keep your elbows off the table and maintain good posture. If dining in a formal restaurant with multiple utensils in the place setting, remember that silverware is used from the outside in.

Funerals

A funeral is not an event people typically like to discuss. However, at some point in your working career, you will need to attend the funeral of a coworker or client.

When a coworker or business associate dies, the relationship you have with that person will dictate if you attend the funeral, send flowers, write a personal card to the family, or perhaps do nothing of a personal nature. Coworkers may send flowers and cards as a group, or the company may send condolences. You may decide these actions are sufficiently respectful. However, culture may influence the ceremonies or traditions the family may request for a funeral. It may be necessary to do some research before you take any actions.

If you choose to attend the visitation, etiquette dictates that proper attire be worn. Appropriate business clothing in dark or muted colors is preferred, but black is not required. When you arrive at the funeral home or before you leave, sign your name on the registry if one has been placed in the entry. If there are many people in attendance, you may need to stand in line in order to talk with the family. There is a possibility that you will not know the family members personally, so introduce yourself as a friend or coworker. It is not necessary to have an extended conversation after the introduction, and a simple "I am sorry for your loss" may be all that is necessary. This statement demonstrates *sympathy* and respect toward the family.

If you attend the funeral, arrive before the service begins and take a seat. Respect the situation and speak softly if you have conversations with others. The funeral ceremony may request attendee participation. If you are uncomfortable participating, it is acceptable to remain silent and respectful.

If you choose to go to the graveside ceremony, follow the instructions that are given for the procession. In general, all drivers should turn on headlights and follow the family cars to the cemetery. If you are not sure of what is expected, it is acceptable to ask the funeral director.

SUMMARY

- **(LO 4-1) Define professional etiquette.**
  Professional etiquette is applying the rules of good manners in the workplace and in other work-related situations. Practicing professional etiquette can help an individual build relationships with coworkers, employers, and customers.
- **(LO 4-2) Cite examples of behaviors that show respect for company workspace.**
  A workspace is the specific area within a company's location where an employee works. Workspace etiquette is the practice of applying the rules of good manners while in an office, cubicle, or the shared working areas of a workplace.
- **(LO 4-3) Identify guidelines for digital devices in the workplace.**
  As a professional, it is important to display good manners and know when to refrain from using digital devices. Phones should be silenced and not visible on the table. A general rule is to turn off digital devices when in a meeting with coworkers.
- **(LO 4-4) Discuss proper business dining etiquette.**
  There may be times when business is discussed over a meal. In this situation, business dining etiquette should be followed. This consists of dressing appropriately, being punctual, and eating politely. Workplace etiquette should be followed.
- **(LO 4-5) Summarize appropriate funeral etiquette.**
  Attending a funeral of a coworker or business associate can be stressful. The level of relationship with the deceased dictates the actions that should be taken.

GLOSSARY TERMS

Visit the G-W Learning companion website at **www.g-wlearning.com/careereducation/** to review the following glossary terms.

protocol   workspace etiquette

REVIEW

1. Define professional etiquette.

2. Cite examples of behaviors that show respect for company workspace.

3. Identify guidelines for digital devices in the workplace.

4. Discuss proper business dining etiquette.

5. Provide examples of appropriate actions that demonstrate respect for the death of a coworker or business associate.

APPLICATION

1. Professional etiquette is applying good manners in the workplace. Figure 4-1 lists examples of proper business etiquette. What additional behaviors would you add to this list that you think should be demonstrated by all employees?

2. One example of professional etiquette is to address people by their names. If a store clerk, waiter or waitress, or other worker is wearing a name tag, it is customary and respectful to call that person by his or her name. Why do you think it is important to use a person's name?

3. What type of personal business would you refrain from sharing with a coworker while at work? What type of personal business do you think is acceptable to discuss with a coworker at work?

4. Recall a time when you may have unintentionally violated workspace etiquette. Describe the incident and the outcome.

5. Workplace etiquette implies that gossip should be avoided. How would you advise a coworker to avoid getting involved in this type of behavior?

6. What actions would you take if you witnessed a coworker violating workplace etiquette?

7. Consider a situation in which you are working in a cubicle and overhear two coworkers talking about a movie they recently saw. The conversation is loud enough for you to hear without eavesdropping, has been going on for more than a few minutes, and has caused you to lose concentration on your work. How would you respond to such a situation?

8. Summarize digital device etiquette that you personally follow.

9. Assume you have organized a business meeting that will be conducted over lunch. The location is a mid-range family restaurant. Attending the meeting will be two coworkers from your team and one outside contractual worker. Describe the etiquette you should assume as host of the meeting.

10. Create a list of several questions about etiquette to which a person might need responses before attending the funeral of a coworker.

INTERNET ACTIVITY

Workplace Disruptions. When office neighbors are loud, it can be nearly impossible to get work done. Conduct an Internet search for suggestions about how to handle a disruptive neighboring coworker. Take note of important tips that could help you in future situations.

SKILLS PRACTICE

Visit the G-W Learning companion website at **www.g-wlearning.com/careereducation/** to access and complete the following soft skills practice activities:

Activity SS4-1 Business Dining. Proper table setting etiquette should be followed at a business dinner. Open the SS4-1 file, and review your knowledge of a dinner place setting.

Activity SS4-2 Shared Workspace Guidelines. Employees are expected to keep company workspaces clean and in order. This is especially true for shared workspaces. Open the SS4-2 file, and create a list of shared workspace guidelines.

Minerva Studio/Shutterstock.com

BEFORE YOU READ

Visit the G-W Learning companion website to view a video about soft skills. The video is available at **www.g-wlearning.com/careereducation/**

LEARNING OUTCOMES

On completion of this chapter, prepare to:

5-1 Evaluate appropriate dress for the workplace.

5-2 Identify appropriate dress for business meetings.

Professional attire is the dress that is dictated by the workplace and appropriate for the job.

bikeriderlondon/Shutterstock.com

Workplace Dress

There are many clichés about career-appropriate dress, such as "dress for the job you want, not for the job you have," "clothes make the person," and "dress for success." Appropriate dress for the workplace shows an individual's professionalism. It is the first thing that makes an impression on people you meet and is one aspect of a professional image over which you have total control.

Each day, ask yourself how you want to be perceived by others. Do you have a meeting of which you are in charge and need to demonstrate your skills or authority? Do you have a day without meetings and will be confined to your workspace for most of the day?

Dress is the type and style of clothing worn. **Professional attire** is the dress that is dictated by the workplace and appropriate for the job. Not everyone wears a suit to work. Many work environments require uniforms or other specific garments that reflect the brand or image that is being projected. Depending on the industry, there may be safety requirements, such as wearing a hard hat or reflective vest. Medical positions may require scrubs or lab coats.

Good grooming complements the dress. It is necessary to shower every day and practice good personal hygiene. For men, facial hair should be neat and trimmed. For women, excessive makeup should be avoided. For both men and women, hairstyles should be appropriate for the work environment, strong perfumes and colognes should be avoided, and jewelry should be kept to a minimum. Tattoos and piercings should not be apparent or distracting.

Your employer's human resources department will have a dress code or guidelines for employees. Rules of dress have relaxed over the years, so an employee should ask for clarification regarding any guidelines that are not clear.

Uniforms

A **uniform** is a prescribed form of dress worn by everybody in a particular group, such as a company or department. Many work environments require employees to wear uniforms, protective clothing, or company clothing, such as a shirt with a company insignia. In these situations, it is important to thoroughly understand the rules of the dress code. Uniforms are often required for health and safety reasons or to make employees of a business easily recognizable to its customers.

If your employer requires you to wear a uniform, follow the rules closely. Bending the rules can result in a safety hazard for yourself or for those around you. If you have any questions about your uniform, consult your supervisor.

For some businesses, jeans are considered the "uniform." If the workplace is casual and jeans are acceptable, dress should still conform to the professional standards dictated by the employer. Clothing should be clean, presentable, and in good taste.

Business-Professional Dress

Business-professional dress is the most formal style of dress in the workplace. The higher an employee's position or rank, the more formal the dress that may be expected. High-profile jobs, such as CEOs, attorneys, and politicians, generally require business-professional dress.

For men, business-professional dress typically means a suit, neutral-color dress shirt, and tie. Dress shoes in black or dark brown are standard. For women, a suit or an appropriate business dress is expected. Dress shoes in subtle colors are preferred, and extremely high heels are generally discouraged.

However, most professional jobs usually do not require the highest level of business-professional dress. For men, a combination of a dress shirt, tie, and dress slacks is usually acceptable as business-professional dress. Sometimes, a sport coat may be required. For women, the standards may be defined more loosely. Dresses, slacks, or skirts with a jacket are examples of acceptable business-professional wear.

Business-Casual Dress

Many employers have adopted a business-casual style of dress. This is more difficult to define than business-professional dress, as it has many interpretations. **Business-casual dress** is dress that is often considered to be "one step down" from business-professional dress. However, it does not mean sloppy dress. Examples of appropriate business-professional and business-casual dress are identified in Figure 5-1. Khakis, long-sleeved shirts, and dress sweaters are examples of business casual for both men and women. Jeans and athletic wear are not considered acceptable business-casual dress.

Jeans Day

A company-wide jeans day is the only day jeans should be worn in a professional workplace. It is a day designated by the company, either a regular day or a special day. This often occurs on a Friday, but may be any day the company chooses. Clothing should always be tasteful and free of messages that are violent, discriminatory, abusive, offensive, demeaning, or otherwise unprofessional in nature.

Figure 5-1 Professional attire is the dress that is dictated by the workplace and appropriate for the job.

Appropriate Dress for the Workplace	
Business-Professional	
Men	**Women**
Dress shirts and ties	Career-style dresses
Suits	Coordinating skirts and blouses
Blazers	Suit jackets and pants
Dress shoes	Dress shoes
Business-Casual	
Men	**Women**
Khaki pants	Casual skirts with knit tops
Button-down shirts, no tie	Khaki pants
Polo-style shirts	Casual-style dresses—not strapless
Casual footwear—no athletic shoes, flip-flops, or sandals	Casual footwear—no athletic shoes, flip-flops, or sandals

Goodheart-Willcox Publisher

Sweatshirts, T-shirts, and tank tops are not appropriate for the workplace, even on jeans day. Shorts are not acceptable. Midriffs should be covered, and provocative clothing should not be worn. Gym shoes are typically not acceptable. Additionally, jeans day is not an excuse to ignore personal hygiene.

Business Meeting Apparel

There are various types of meetings conducted during a business day. Generally, routine company meetings with coworkers do not require special dress. The daily dress code for the business is acceptable unless otherwise noted.

Case Study

chrisdorney/Shutterstock.com

Workplace Dress Code

In August 2014, Walmart announced that it was changing its employee dress code. The company said that it would still supply the signature blue vests to its employees, but employees would be required to wear collared shirts and khakis with the vests provided. The cost for new attire would be at the employees' expense. The goal of this decision was to promote a more professional look for the company, but it was met with hostility from employees. Workers stated that they are not paid enough to buy new clothes specifically for work, and many have asked that the company supply the clothing for its employees. Federal laws regarding uniforms state that, depending on the situation, a company may be required to pay the bill for the purchase and maintenance of employee uniforms. However, since Walmart called this a "dress code," those laws may not apply. It would seem the company simply assumed that everyone had collared shirts and khakis already in his or her wardrobe, but such a generalization may not always be a reality.

1. Suggest an appropriate strategy that employees should use to discuss conflict with management about dress code.

2. Discuss the importance of employee participation or nonparticipation in a company's decision to change a dress code.

3. Why do you think a company would prefer a dress code for its employees?

4. Discuss the issue of who pays for specific clothing required by a dress code. Should it be the employer or the employee if the clothing is not a safety requirement of the job?

Meetings in which people from outside the business are invited as guests dictate that business-professional dress be worn by employees who host the meeting. Employees represent the company and its brand as well as the individual's professional image.

The guests or hosts of a meeting can also set the standard for dress of those in attendance. Some cultures expect business-professional dress for their employees. For example, Japanese culture dictates business suits for men and women for all professional activities. When attending or hosting a meeting that includes people from other countries or cultures, research the dress that shows respect.

When attending conferences or meetings away from company property, the protocol for attire may be business-professional or business-casual. Conference information will generally state acceptable dress. When in doubt, be conservative. Meetings provide networking opportunities, and appropriate dress is, once again, part of a company's image as well as your professional image.

Off-site business events may suggest resort or casual wear as the dress for the occasion. This does not mean jeans or shorts but casual clothing such as khaki pants, polo-style shirt, and a sweater. Examples of types of apparel that are never appropriate in the workplace or at work events are listed in Figure 5-2.

Many work environments require employees to wear protective clothing.

Dmitry Kalinovsky/Shutterstock.com

Figure 5-2 Certain types of clothing and accessories are never appropriate in a professional environment.

Inappropriate Apparel for the Workplace

- Workout or athletic clothing
- Ball caps, unless part of the uniform
- Flip-flops or sandals
- Jeans with rips or holes
- Shorts
- Tops that are cropped or too revealing
- Clothing that is unclean
- T-shirts and tank tops
- Clothing with offensive graphics
- Frayed or worn clothing

Goodheart-Willcox Publisher

SUMMARY

- **(LO 5-1) Evaluate appropriate dress for the workplace.**
  Dress is the first thing that makes an impression on the people you meet. It is one aspect of a professional image over which an individual has total control. Depending on the industry and your position, appropriate dress may be business-professional, business-casual, or a uniform.

- **(LO 5-2) Identify appropriate dress for business meetings.**
  The attendees, location, and event type should be considered when choosing appropriate dress for a meeting. Meetings provide networking opportunities, and appropriate dress is part of the company's image and an individual's professional image, as well.

GLOSSARY TERMS

Visit the G-W Learning companion website at **www.g-wlearning.com/careereducation/** to review the following glossary terms.

business-casual dress	professional attire
business-professional dress	uniform

REVIEW

1. Evaluate appropriate dress for the workplace.

2. List examples of reasons why a uniform may be required.

3. Explain the difference between business-professional dress and business-casual dress.

4. Describe appropriate attire for a company-wide jeans day.

5. Identify criteria that should be used when deciding dress for a business meeting.

APPLICATION

1. What does the expression "dress for the job you want, not for the job you have" mean to you?

2. Describe the type of apparel you typically wear for a casual day at work or school.

3. List examples of reasons why you think an employer would not want employees to have tattoos or piercings, even if it does not affect job performance.

4. Summarize your opinion about dress codes and the impact they have on employee morale.

5. Describe the dress of a coworker who is always dressed *appropriately* for the workplace.

6. Describe the dress of a coworker who is always dressed *inappropriately* for the workplace.

7. Explain how the dress and appearance of a coworker influences your opinion of that person's professional image.

8. What is the appropriate dress for your current job? Is the dress considered to be professional or business casual?

9. Over the last few decades, dress code in the workplace has become more relaxed. Why do you think this is the trend?

10. Describe the appropriate dress for a formal business meeting that is held off-site from your workplace.

INTERNET ACTIVITY

Professional Dress. Dress is a direct reflection of professional image. Visit your employer's or school's website and navigate to the *about* information. What type of dress do you think a potential employee or student would perceive to be acceptable based on the information posted on that web page?

SKILLS PRACTICE

Visit the G-W Learning companion website at **www.g-wlearning.com/careereducation/** to access and complete the following soft skills practice activities:

Activity SS5-1 Dress Code. Most places of employment have an employee dress code. Open the SS5-1 file, read the document, and then summarize any suggestions you would make in the document if you were responsible for the dress code.

Activity SS5-2 Selecting Appropriate Dress. Professionals select appropriate dress for all occasions that are related to business. Open the SS5-2 file, and identify appropriate dress for each situation.

CHAPTER 6

Communication Skills

Stephen Coburn/Shutterstock.com

BEFORE YOU READ

Visit the G-W Learning companion website to view a video about soft skills. The video is available at **www.g-wlearning.com/careereducation/**

LEARNING OUTCOMES

On completion of this chapter, prepare to:

6-1   Define communication and the communication process.

6-2   Explain the importance of language and its effects on communication.

Communication is the process of using words, sounds, signs, or actions to exchange information and express thoughts.

adriaticfoto/Shutterstock.com

Communication

Communication is the process of using words, sounds, signs, or actions to exchange information and express thoughts. It is how we talk and listen to others. Communication skills affect your basic ability to understand others, establish positive relationships, and perform in most situations. Being able to communicate skillfully, therefore, is essential to your ability to succeed in your career.

Informal communication is casual sharing of information with no customs or rules of etiquette involved. An example is having a conversation with a friend or family member. *Formal communication* is sharing of information that conforms to specific protocol. *Protocol* is a set of customs or rules of etiquette. Formal communication is planned, rather than spontaneous, and is delivered as a written or spoken message.

When people communicate, there is a specific reason for doing so. There are five basic purposes of communication, as shown in Figure 6-1.

Soft skills play an important role in the effectiveness of all communication, regardless of how or why it is delivered. There is a process that applies to any type of communication, as well as ways to overcome communication barriers that may occur.

Communication Process

All communication follows the same basic process. The **communication process** is a series of actions on the part of the sender and the receiver of a message, as well as the path the message follows. The six elements of the communication process are the sender, message, channel, receiver, translation, and feedback, as shown in Figure 6-2.

The person who has a message to communicate is called the *sender*. The sender decides there is a need to relay information to the receiver. He or she also decides what information to send.

The information to be relayed is the *message*. **Encoding** is the process of turning the idea for a message into symbols that can be communicated. The sender might choose to use written or spoken words, static images, dynamic visuals, such as a YouTube video, or any combination of these. Most people convert their messages into a language of written or spoken words or symbols the receiver can understand.

Once the message is encoded, it is ready to be sent. The act of sending a message is called **transmission**. The **channel**, also known as *medium*, is how the message is transmitted, such as face-to-face, telephone, text, or other vehicle that is appropriate for the situation.

The *receiver* is the person who reads, hears, or sees the message. This is the person for whom the sender created the message. He or she, or the group, is known as the *audience* of the message.

Figure 6-1 The purpose of communication usually falls into one of the categories listed in this table.

Purposes of Communication

- **Inform.** A message that informs is one that provides information or education.
- **Persuade.** A message that persuades is one that attempts to change the behavior of the receiver.
- **Instruct.** A message that instructs others is one that attempts to provide direction or guidance.
- **Make a request.** A message that makes a request is one that asks a question about information or asks for an action to occur.
- **Respond to a request.** A message that responds to a request is one that provides the information requested.

Goodheart-Willcox Publisher

Figure 6-2 The communication process is a series of actions on the part of the sender and the receiver of a message, as well as the path the message follows.

Communication Process

Sender → Message → Channel → Receiver → Translation → Feedback

Goodheart-Willcox Publisher

Once the receiver has the message, it is translated into terms the receiver can understand. The process of translation is called **decoding**.

Feedback is the receiver's response to the sender, and it concludes the communication process. If the sender does not receive feedback to be sure the message was understood, the communication process has failed.

Communication Barriers

The communication process seems relatively straightforward. However, the failure to use soft skills can create barriers, and the end result can be disastrous. A *barrier* is anything that prevents clear, effective communication. Barriers may occur in any type of communication and may be present during sending or receiving.

Sending Barriers

A *sending barrier* is present when the sender says or does something that causes the receiver to stop listening to or reading a message. This can happen when the receiver simply does not understand what the sender is communicating. If the message is written, barriers may include poor grammar or spelling, typographical and formatting errors, and inappropriate language. If the message is verbal, barriers may include distracting mannerisms, facial expressions that conflict with the words being said, and inappropriate dress or demeanor.

Receiving Barriers

A *receiving barrier* is present when the receiver says or does something that causes the sender's message not to be received. While *hearing* is a physical ability, *listening* is a conscious action. If the receiver is not actively listening to the sender or reading the written message, the communication process breaks down. Receiving barriers can be just as harmful to the communication process as sending barriers.

Language

When you send a message, you select language and construct sentences in a way that will achieve your purpose. The way in which you use language can have a major effect on communication. *Formal language* is language that is used in a workplace environment and requires use of Standard English. **Standard English** refers to English language usage that follows accepted rules for word use, pronunciation, spelling, grammar, and punctuation.

Informal communication is casual sharing of information with no customs or rules of etiquette involved.

g-stockstudio/Shutterstock.com

Informal language is language used in a casual situation. It is characterized by the use of contractions, lack of relative pronouns with relative clauses, and the use of omitted or implied material. Most people use informal language with friends and family. Spoken language is usually informal, although a speech or lecture is likely conducted using formal language.

Words have exact meaning according to the dictionary, or **denotation**. Another term is **explicit** meaning. Sometimes words convey meanings outside of their definition and vary according to the context in which they are used. **Context** is the environment in which something occurs or the surrounding information that is communicated. **Tone** is an impression of the content of the message. Is it friendly or hostile, demanding or courteous, sensitive or insensitive? Tone is how words are interpreted by the receiver.

In some cases, however, context and tone are not enough. The real meaning of words resides in the mind of the receiver. The **connotation** of a word is its meaning apart from what it explicitly names or describes. The meaning is implied

Case Study

Communication Skills

Helga Esteb/Shutterstock.com

On January 14, 2016, the nominees for the 88th Academy Awards were announced. For the second consecutive year, there were no minority nominees in the acting categories and only one minority nominee in the directing category. This was met with social backlash from minority communities who encouraged celebrities and fans to boycott the ceremonies. Members of the Academy defended the nominations, saying that nominations are merit-based and the result of voting. They claimed that having minority actors, actresses, and directors on the ballots proved that race is not a problem. One week after the nominations were announced, Cheryl Boone Isaacs, the sitting president of the Academy, announced changes to voting eligibility, stating, "The Academy is going to lead and not wait for the industry to catch up; these new measures … will have an immediate impact and begin the process of significantly changing our membership composition."

1. Describe the tone of Isaacs's communication.

2. How would you describe Cheryl Boone Isaacs's leadership?

3. Explain the level of cultural awareness Isaacs demonstrated by promising to change the Academy's membership composition.

4. What effect did Cheryl Boone Isaacs's announcement about the Academy have on her professional image?

or **implicit**. For example, the primary definition of *foreign* is something outside of one's own country. However, to some people, the word has a negative connotation. The word *foreign* can be implied as *other*, meaning *not one of us* or *not like us*. In the workplace, the word *international* is most often used in place of the word *foreign*.

Words should be chosen that suit the situation in which they are used. Certain types of words and phrases are not appropriate to use in every situation. Slang should not be used in business communication. *Slang* is words and phrases that are not considered part of Standard English. Texting language, such as using the letter *u* instead of the word *you*, is not acceptable in business. Additionally, condescending words, biased words, jargon, clichés, and euphemisms should not be used.

Condescending Words

Language that is condescending should be avoided. To be *condescending* means to assume an attitude of superiority. Words should be used that can be understood, but not interpreted to mean superiority. An explanation that is too basic to make sure the listener understands may be condescending. The receiver's level of knowledge on a topic should be considered to avoid insulting a person's intelligence.

Biased Words

It is important to use language free of bias. A *bias* is a tendency to believe that some ideas or people are better than others, which often results in acting unfairly. Biased words are those that can identify a personal characteristic about someone, such as gender, ethnicity, or age, often in a demeaning or hurtful manner. **Bias-free words** are neutral words that impart neither a positive nor negative message.

For example, bias-free words do not reveal personal characteristics about an individual. Using gender-neutral words, such as *server* rather than *waiter* or *waitress*, focuses on the job or the individual's qualifications instead of the gender of the individual. Rather than saying, "We hired a *young man* for the manager job," state, "We hired a *new manager*."

When a disability must be referenced, a specific term, such as *hearing impaired* or *physical disability*, should be used. It is inappropriate to use outdated terms that are now considered offensive.

Jargon and Clichés

Various professions and industries have specific words and phrases that are familiar to those who work in those fields. **Jargon** is technical terminology or vocabulary specific to a field of work or group. These terms are sometimes considered *insider vocabulary* and may not be understood by those outside the field. For example, stockbrokers talk about *bull* and *bear* markets. Retailers talk about *retail*, *wholesale*, and *markdown prices*. These terms may not be readily understandable for those who do not work in finance or retail. Jargon should be used sparingly and only when it applies to a situation.

Clichés are overused, commonplace, or trite language. Often, clichés are not well received. In some cases, the true meaning of the cliché may not be apparent, or the cliché may mean one thing to one person and something different to another person.

Euphemisms

Some words may sound acceptable in conversation, but may come across as harsh in writing. For those words, you may need to find a euphemism. A **euphemism** is a word that expresses unpleasant ideas in more pleasant terms. For example, years ago, the *customer service department* was commonly called the *customer complaint office*. The new term reflects the desire of a business to service customers' needs, but the purpose of the department is still to solve issues or complaints that customers may have. Some businesses even use the term *customer care* to communicate greater sensitivity to the customer's needs. Euphemisms should be used when needed but used wisely. The use of euphemisms to intentionally hide the true meaning or to distract the receiver should be avoided.

SUMMARY

- **(LO 6-1) Define communication and the communication process.**
  Communication is the process of using words, sounds, signs, or actions to exchange information or express thoughts. It is how we talk and listen to others. Communication skills affect a person's basic ability to understand others, establish positive relationships, and perform in most situations. The communication process is used to inform, persuade, instruct, make a request, and respond to a request. The communication process consists of a series of actions on the part of the sender and the receiver of a message and the path the message follows.

- **(LO 6-2) Explain the importance of language and its effects on communication.**
  When a writer sends a message, language is selected and constructed in sentences in a way that achieves the writer's purpose. The way in which language is used can have a major effect on communication. Language may be formal or informal. To ensure success of all communication, words should be chosen that suit the situation in which they are used and condescending words, biased words, jargon, clichés, and euphemisms should be avoided.

GLOSSARY TERMS

Visit the G-W Learning companion website at **www.g-wlearning.com/careereducation/** to review the following glossary terms.

bias-free words	euphemism
channel	explicit
communication	feedback
communication process	implicit
connotation	jargon
context	Standard English
decoding	tone
denotation	transmission
encoding	

REVIEW

1. Define communication.

2. List the six elements of the communication process.

3. Explain sending barriers and receiving barriers that occur during the communication process.

4. Explain the importance of language and its effects on communication.

5. List examples of guidelines that should be followed when making word choices.

APPLICATION

1. Describe the protocol you personally follow when participating in formal communication.

2. Figure 6-1 lists five basic purposes of communication. Write an example of a message that addresses each purpose.

3. Identify ways a receiver can give feedback to the sender of a message.

4. There are many communication barriers that can occur on the part of the sender. Identify several barriers that could have a negative impact on a message that you send to another person.

5. Communication barriers can occur on the part of the receiver. Identify several barriers that could cause the message not to be understood by the receiver.

6. Describe what the expression "it is not what you say, but how you say it" means to you.

7. How would you respond to a person who uses condescending language while in conversation with you?

8. Describe a situation in which you witnessed a person using biased language toward another person. How did this conversation impact your opinion of the person who used the inappropriate language?

9. Discuss the potential outcome of a conversation that uses jargon and clichés of an industry with which the receiver is unfamiliar.

10. Make a list of the jargon used by your profession or career interest.

INTERNET ACTIVITY

English as a Second Language. Being able to communicate skillfully is essential to your ability to succeed in your career. In the workplace, you will communicate with many people for whom English is their second language. Research English as a second language (ESL) and ways that, if in conversation with someone whose first language is not English, you can avoid communication barriers.

SKILLS PRACTICE

Visit the G-W Learning companion website at **www.g-wlearning.com/careereducation/** to access and complete the following soft skills practice activities:

Activity SS6-1 Word Choice. Words should be chosen that suit the situation in which they are used. To review your understanding of certain words, open the SS6-1 file, and complete the charts that include synonyms, antonyms, analogies, and context.

Activity SS6-2 Business Jargon. Jargon is technical terminology or vocabulary specific to a field of work or group. It should only be used when the audience understands the lingo. To review your understanding of business jargon, open the SS6-2 file, and translate the meaning of each business jargon term.

Activity SS6-3 Misused Words. Many words in the English language are often confused with other words or simply misused. Open the SS6-3 file, and select the correct words for the paragraphs.

Verbal and Nonverbal Communication

Syda Productions/Shutterstock.com

BEFORE YOU READ

Visit the G-W Learning companion website to view a video about soft skills. The video is available at **www.g-wlearning.com/careereducation/**

LEARNING OUTCOMES

On completion of this chapter, prepare to:

7-1   Explain verbal communication.

7-2   List examples of nonverbal communication.

Public speaking is speaking to a large group.

g-stockstudio/Shutterstock.com

Verbal Communication

Verbal communication is speaking words to communicate. Verbal communication allows information to be shared, requests to be made, direction to be given, and persuasion to be applied when action is needed—all without having to write down the messages. There are many instances during a typical day when you are required to communicate verbally. In every situation and conversation, confident verbal communication conveys who you are as a professional.

The **verbal communication process** is a series of actions on the part of the sender and the receiver of a message. The primary communication happens on the part of the speaker. The person sending the message must make sure the words used are clear so the receiver understands what is being transmitted. The speaker's voice must be clear and understandable, as the voice is the channel in the process. The receiver then decodes or translates the message into terms that he or she can understand.

Words

As discussed in Chapter 6, words are the tools of verbal communication. You must plan and organize your thoughts to select the appropriate words for the message. This might be as simple as thinking before you speak. It could also be as elaborate as researching and outlining a presentation and practicing several times before you deliver it. Planning involves thinking about who will receive the message and what you want to accomplish. Making notes before a phone call, having an agenda for a meeting, or researching information in advance are all methods that can be used to prepare before talking to people at work in the workplace.

Voice

Voice is the channel for verbal communication. Naturally, your voice is your most important tool in speaking situations. Your voice and *how* you convey words are almost as important as *what* you say. *Tone* is an impression of the overall content of the message. It is easier to get results by expressing a positive tone rather than a negative one. For example, it is always better to emphasize what you *can* do rather than what you *cannot* do. Many words tend to automatically bring about negative reactions. Similarly, there are words that generally have a positive effect.

If you speak too loudly or too softly, listeners will be distracted from the content of your message. The listener will quickly tune out what you are saying, so you must adjust your volume to the situation. In general, maintain a consistent, normal rate. If you talk too slowly or too quickly, you may lose the attention of the listener. You can vary your rate of speed for emphasis. However, when presenting something technical or complicated, you should talk slowly. Another effective speaking technique is simply to pause so the word or phrase following the pause receives extra emphasis.

You can stress a word to make it stand out from the others by simply increasing the volume of your voice. **Modulation** is changing the emphasis of words by raising and lowering your voice. You can also provide emphasis by changing the pitch of your voice. **Pitch** describes the highness or lowness of a sound. **Intonation** is the rise and fall in the pitch of your voice.

Mispronounced words are a distraction and may even affect your credibility. In some cases, you might be more familiar with a word in writing than you are with saying it aloud. Regional differences in speech or English not being a person's native language might also contribute to different pronunciation. Common errors in pronunciation are shown in Figure 7-1. Another factor in the audience understanding what you say is **enunciation**, which is clearly and distinctly pronouncing syllables and sounds.

When engaging in conversation, pause and ask for feedback before changing the subject. Look for visual cues that a listener wants to respond, such as opening his or her mouth to speak. Always be courteous, and refrain from talking over or interrupting others. Provide your listener with the opportunity to respond to what you are saying.

Speaking Situations

There are many speaking situations that happen within the workday. **Impromptu speaking** is talking without advance notice or an opportunity to plan what will be said. It is important to react with professionalism in these speaking situations. Take a moment to think about what you are going to say. If someone asks for complex information, you can say, "I will get back to you." If you do not have the answer, courteously direct the person to another source for the information.

Figure 7-1 Mispronounced words are a distraction to a listener and can affect a speaker's credibility.

Common Errors in Pronunciation

Dropping Sounds at the End of Words

For example, do you drop the *g* in *ing* words and say *runnin'*, *eatin'*, or *workin'*? Do you drop the final *t* when you say words such as list and tourist? Do you drop the final *d* in words such as field and build?

Omitting Letters and Sounds

For example, consider the word introduce. The correct pronunciation is IN-tro-duce, not IN-ter-duce.

Adding Sounds

For example, do you say ATH-a-lete? The correct pronunciation is ATH-lete.

Altering Vowel Sounds

For example, do you say GEN-you-in (correct) or GEN-you-ine (incorrect)?

Stressing the Wrong Syllable

For example, you should say in-COM-pa-ra-ble, not in-com-PAR-a-ble, and in-SUR-ance, not IN-sur-ance.

Mispronouncing Words

Many people make the mistake of pronouncing words just as they appear in writing. For example, do you pronounce the word epitome as i-PIT-i-me (correct) or I-pi-tome (incorrect)?

Using Incorrect Words

For example, for the verb form of orientation, do you say orient (correct) or orientate (incorrect)?

Goodheart-Willcox Publisher

Body language is nonverbal messages sent through gestures, facial expressions, and posture.

Mila Supinskaya Glashchenko

The goal is to always respond with professionalism in a positive and intelligent manner. Impromptu speaking is common in interpersonal communication. *Interpersonal communication* is communication that occurs between the sender and one other person.

A **group discussion** is a speaking situation in which three or more individuals share their ideas about a subject. It is also known as *small group communication*. Group discussions are often informative or persuasive. Similar to brainstorming, ideas are given without any judgment. When speaking freely and sharing ideas, words should be chosen carefully and professional protocol followed.

Public speaking is generally communication delivered to a large group from a podium and with a microphone. It may also be referred to as *public communication*. The communication is often planned and carefully composed as a speech or presentation. Public speaking is generally more formal than impromptu speaking or group discussions.

Nonverbal Communication

People with good soft skills are able to control their nonverbal communication to coincide with and complement their messages. **Nonverbal communication** is any action, behavior, or attitude that sends a message to the receiver. It includes body language, eye contact, touch, personal space, and paralanguage. It is often used in conjunction with verbal communication. Nonverbal communication can be so strong that it overwhelms the verbal message. For example, if someone stops by your office to talk and you say you are not busy, but you keep scrolling through your mailbox, your body language sends a message implying you *are* busy.

Some nonverbal messages are subtle. For example, jingling keys or coins in your pockets during a conversation is distracting and can suggest that you are bored with or uninterested in the conversation. Other messages involve behavior that sends loud messages in spite of what you might say. For example, if you visit a client's office and leave your coat on while standing near the door, the client is going to receive the message that you are in a hurry to leave.

As with any communication, nonverbal messages must be considered in the context in which they occur. For example, a smile can mean a person finds your statement funny or it could mean he or she does not believe you. Context is used to determine what the nonverbal message actually means.

Body Language

Body language is nonverbal messages sent through gestures, facial expressions, and posture. If you smile, sneer, raise an eyebrow, shrug your shoulders, nod your head, cross your arms, or clench your teeth, you are communicating a message just as if you were talking. The receiver picks up on these cues, and the cues become an important part of your message. This is why being aware of body language is an essential professional skill. In a workplace environment, you must be aware of the nonverbal messages you send and receive. Otherwise, you run the risk of sending the wrong message or feedback.

Eye Contact

In every culture, eye contact is an important form of nonverbal communication. In American culture, appropriate eye contact means looking directly at the other person, but not staring too intensely, while engaged in conversation. Staring may make the other person uncomfortable. In some cultures, however, it may be considered rude to make eye contact when speaking or listening.

Most people have a natural tendency to look directly at the person with whom they are engaged in conversation. What if someone approaches you while you are in the middle of doing something, such as dialing a telephone or reading an e-mail? If you do not stop what you are doing and make eye contact, you are saying, "Please go away; I'm too busy to talk to you now."

A distracted listener may allow his or her eyes to roam the room, not realizing that the speaker interprets the wandering eyes as disinterest or disdain. Being more aware of your own body language is the only way to prevent these kinds of unintended messages.

Touch

Touch is another form of nonverbal communication that sends strong messages. *Haptics communication* is nonverbal communication that occurs through touch. A firm handshake, along with eye contact and a smile, sends an important message when you are introduced to someone new. These gestures convey openness and confidence. Open and confident body language in professional situations helps create the impression of someone who is competent and trustworthy.

In the workplace, a handshake is about the only form of touch that is acceptable. Any other form of physical contact must be within the boundaries of professional appropriateness. These boundaries vary, depending on the nature of the business and the culture. For example, a dentist must touch your face in order to complete an examination. However, if you were working in an office and somebody touched your face, you would be very upset, if not offended. In general, avoid participation in any physical contact other than what is required of your work.

Personal Space

Personal space is the physical space between two individuals. How you identify your personal space and the judgment you apply to the space of others varies depending on your social upbringing and community norms.

The reaction of the person with whom you are conversing can be affected by how close you stand or sit to him or her. The personal-space boundary is difficult to notice, but becomes apparent when someone violates it. Figure 7-2 illustrates generally accepted personal space guidelines for different relationships.

Cultural background may be a factor in defining the personal-space boundary. For example, Americans tend to keep a slightly greater distance between themselves and others than do people from some other cultures.

Figure 7-2 Personal space is the physical space between two individuals, and its boundaries only become apparent when someone gets too close.

Personal Space Guidelines

3–10 feet for coworkers

> 4 feet for strangers

> 12 feet for speaking to a large group

Goodheart-Willcox Publisher

Paralanguage

Paralanguage is the attitude projected with the tone and pitch of a person's voice. It is communication separate from language. It is reflected in speech as a sharp or soft tone, raising or lowering of the voice, speaking quickly or slowly, and the general quality of the voice. Paralanguage is nonverbal communication that reflects an individual's true attitude, so it is important to be aware of it. When the content of your message is contradicted by the attitude with which you are communicating, your message will be received accordingly. If you say you are not angry, but you raise your voice, the receiver will know you really *are* angry.

Whenever you are speaking, remember that the tone, pitch, quality of voice, and rate of speaking convey emotions that will be assessed by the receiver, regardless of the message's content. The voice is not just a vehicle for the message; it is part of the message. A good communicator is sensitive to the influence of paralanguage on the interpretation of the message by the receiver. When your voice complements the message, there is a greater chance that your words will be received as you intended.

WWW.ANSAFRICA.ORG

Tinseltown/Shutterstock.com

Case Study

Verbal Communication

Archbishop Desmond Tutu is a South African social rights activist who came to worldwide prominence in the 1980s through his opposition of apartheid. He has received many respected humanitarian and peace awards, including the Nobel Peace Prize in 1984. He continues to be active in social issues, including poverty, racism, and sexism, among other issues. In November of 2004, he gave an address at the Nelson Mandela Foundation in Johannesburg, South Africa. He commented on the slow pace of economic redistribution in South Africa, as well as the government's policies on other issues. In reference to politicians and activists trying to persuade the other side, Tutu's message was that everyone involved in the discussion should be able to communicate without resorting to shouting matches and muckraking. He said, "Don't raise your voice; improve your argument." Since then, this quote has been used as inspiration for proper discussion and communication in situations as varied as negotiations and sales messages.

1. What do you think is the meaning of the quote, "Don't raise your voice; improve your argument"?

2. How does Tutu's quote apply to nonverbal communication as well as verbal communication?

3. Describe what can be learned about etiquette from Tutu's message of "communicate without resorting to shouting matches and muckraking."

4. How would you describe Desmond Tutu's professional image?

SUMMARY

- **(LO 7-1) Explain verbal communication.**
  Verbal communication is speaking words to communicate. It allows information to be shared, requests to be made, direction to be given, and persuasion to be applied when action is needed, all without having to write down the messages.
- **(LO 7-2) List examples of nonverbal communication.**
  Nonverbal communication can be demonstrated through any action, behavior, or attitude that sends a message to the receiver. It includes body language, attention to personal space, behavior, and attitude.

GLOSSARY TERMS

Visit the G-W Learning companion website at **www.g-wlearning.com/careereducation/** to review the following glossary terms.

body language	nonverbal communication
enunciation	paralanguage
group discussion	pitch
impromptu speaking	public speaking
intonation	verbal communication process
modulation	

REVIEW

1. Define verbal communication and the verbal communication process.

2. In what way are words the tools of verbal communication?

3. List examples of speaking situations that an individual might encounter in the workplace.

4. Describe nonverbal communication.

5. How can a person demonstrate nonverbal communication?

APPLICATION

1. You participate in verbal communication on a daily basis. However, the verbal communication process often breaks down for one reason or another. Identify situations you have encountered in a business conversation that involved misunderstandings of the message.

2. Describe a situation in which the tone of your voice did not match your message. Describe how your audience responded.

3. Read the negative messages that follow. Rewrite each message with a positive tone.
   A. I was not able to make my presentation because the equipment was broken.

   B. My boss did not tell me that the project was due by Friday.

   C. The training program did not provide me with that material.

   D. The transit cost for our clients is too high.

4. Most everyone has words that prove challenging to enunciate or pronounce. Identify words with which you have problems pronouncing or enunciating.

5. Three speaking situations you may encounter in the workplace are impromptu speaking, group discussion, and public speaking. Identify the speaking situation that is the most comfortable and least comfortable for you. Explain why.

6. Recall a time when a person's nonverbal communication made a negative impression on you. Describe the situation and identify if it was body language, eye contact, invasion of personal space, or other nonverbal actions. Explain why you were uncomfortable with the encounter.

7. Some people are more comfortable with eye contact than others. Describe a situation in which you spoke with someone who made little-to-no eye contact with you. Note how the lack of eye contact affected the conversation and why you think the person may not have been making eye contact.

8. What forms of physical contact from a coworker are acceptable? What forms of physical contact are unacceptable?

9. Explain the boundaries you have established for your personal space.

10. Describe a situation in which you were talking with someone and the verbal message didn't match the person's behavior.

INTERNET ACTIVITY

Nonverbal Communication. It is inevitable that someday in your professional career you will work with a person who is a native of another country. Select a country other than the United States and conduct an Internet search for the accepted nonverbal communication in that culture. How do they interpret handshakes, eye contact, and personal space?

SKILLS PRACTICE

Visit the G-W Learning companion website at **www.g-wlearning.com/careereducation/** to access and complete the following soft skills practice activities:

Activity SS7-1 Tone. Tone is an impression of the overall content of a message and can affect the meaning of a message as well as the reaction to it. Open the SS7-1 file, and rewrite the negative statements to create statements with a positive tone.

Activity SS7-2 Nonverbal Communication. Nonverbal communication can be so strong that it overwhelms the verbal message. Open the SS7-2 file, and translate what specific nonverbal actions imply to a person with whom you are having a conversation.

CHAPTER 8

Speaking Skills

racorn/Shutterstock.com

BEFORE YOU READ

Visit the G-W Learning companion website to view a video about soft skills. The video is available at **www.g-wlearning.com/careereducation/**

LEARNING OUTCOMES

On completion of this chapter, prepare to:

8-1   Demonstrate how to make introductions in a professional situation.

8-2   Explain protocol for handling business telephone calls.

8-3   Describe how to conduct a formal meeting.

Introductions

At some point in your personal and professional life, you will be called on to make introductions. An **introduction** is making a person known to someone else by sharing the person's name and other relevant information. You may have to introduce coworkers, managers, or customers to each other. A proper introduction can create a positive first impression, and a negative impression can be created if protocol is not followed. When making professional introductions, the *situation* might be informal, but the *language* should always be formal and appropriate for the workplace.

Introducing Yourself

In both social and professional settings, there will be occasions to introduce yourself to a person you have just met. Introducing yourself exhibits friendliness and confidence. In a professional setting, proper etiquette is to tell the person your full name and your role in the company. For example, a person might introduce herself by saying, "Hello, my name is Madison Gomez; I am a multimedia artist for XYZ Company."

If the person is in rank above you, use professional protocol. Using a title like "Mr." or "Ms." or "Mrs." may be appropriate. When the other party gives his or her name, repeat the person's name as you greet him or her. "It is great to meet you, Mr. Alexander," is a polite way to respond when being introduced to someone in a professional situation. Saying a person's name after being introduced will help you remember it. Remembering a person's name is important to career success. A person generally responds well to the use of his or her name.

Always stand when introducing yourself or introducing others. Professionals extend their hand when meeting a person for the first time, as well as when greeting people they already know. In the United States, handshakes are customary when greeting both men and women. A customary handshake is performed by two people extending their right hands and grasping the other person's hand firmly. Applying the right amount of pressure is important, as a handshake that is too strong makes a person seem overbearing and rude, while a handshake that is too weak makes a person seem timid or submissive.

When you approach someone you may have met before but do not know well, introduce yourself again. This saves embarrassment for all parties if names have been forgotten. Doing so puts everyone at ease and shows you are a professional.

Introducing Others

When introducing two people to each other, clearly say each person's full name. Professional protocol is to introduce the lower-ranking person to the higher-ranking person. If you are introducing a new intern to an executive, you would say: "Tyler, this is Ms. Anita Ogawa, vice president. Anita, this is Tyler Lombard. Tyler is working as our marketing intern this summer."

Try to offer more information to help the two people easily make conversation. For example, you might say: "Clark Morgan, I would like to introduce you to Olivia Price. Olivia is a set designer for the local theater. She has a great idea about how we can improve our merchandise displays."

Professionals extend their hand when meeting a person for the first time, as well as when greeting people they already know.

pikselstock/Shutterstock.com

Introducing Speakers

On occasion, you may make a formal introduction for a person who is the speaker at an event. If you are introducing another person as a speaker, request information about the person in advance. Use the information to develop your introduction. Select information from the speaker's notes that will complement the presentation to be made. Write the points that you wish to express on an index card so that you do not forget to include them. Be specific with what you convey to the audience. For example, you might say what city the person is from or where he or she went to college.

Conversely, you could be the speaker and required to make your own introduction. If you are introducing yourself, give a brief background of who you are and why you are making a presentation. Keep it short, but interesting. This time should not be used as a bragging session.

Case Study

Cheryle Revias/US Army Special Operations Command

Speaking

Anthony Muñoz is an NFL Hall of Fame lineman who retired after spending thirteen seasons playing for the Cincinnati Bengals. After retiring from football in 1993, he became a sports analyst and commentator, but remained active in supporting causes that were important to him. In 2002, he combined all his charitable efforts and established the Anthony Muñoz Foundation. The mission of the non-profit organization is centered on engaging the Cincinnati Tri-State region to impact youth mentally, physically, and spiritually.

His message to the world is "… I'm trying to live a legacy, and be known someday not just as a guy who played for the Bengals. But as someone who loves his community." In fact, former Bengal Coach Sam Wyche commented that "Anthony is a better person than he was a player, and he was one of the greatest players of all time. That is what heroes are supposed to look like."

1. Anthony Muñoz is one of many NFL players who are involved in charitable organizations. What is the message that these players convey about their integrity when they participate in these organizations?

2. Explain how creating the Anthony Muñoz Foundation was a demonstration of Anthony's leadership abilities.

3. Describe what you think the tone of his message conveys when he says "… I'm trying to live a legacy…"

4. What is your opinion of the professional image Muñoz has created?

These types of introductions may require you to approach a stage and use a microphone. As a professional, you should remain calm, project your voice, and show enthusiasm. However, many individuals become nervous when called on a stage to make introductions using a microphone. If these traits do not come to you naturally, consider taking a workshop to help develop them. If a workshop is not practical, practice speaking in front of friends or family and solicit feedback from them. Repeated practice will help you build confidence.

When making an introduction from a stage, remain calm, project your voice, and show enthusiasm.

lightpoet/Shutterstock.com

Telephone Calls

Telephone calls are an essential part of communication in the workplace. Whether you are placing or receiving a telephone call, remember that you are representing your company. It is important to learn the guidelines and etiquette that your organization has in place for using the telephone.

Telephone etiquette is using good manners when speaking on the telephone. Always be courteous to the person on the other end of the call. Be aware of the volume and tone of your voice. Smile when you are talking on the phone; it will make your voice sound more pleasant.

A caller should only be placed on speaker if the phone call requires it. Using speakers on a call can be annoying as they can create an echo that alters the caller's voice and distracts the person on the other end. A speaker should be reserved for conference calls that involve multiple participants.

Callers should not be placed on hold unless absolutely necessary. Being placed on hold is offensive to the person on the other end. If the situation requires that a call be placed on hold, explain why you are leaving the conversation and that you will return as quickly as possible.

Telephone etiquette includes returning phone calls promptly. When someone calls and requests a return call, do so as soon as possible. Industry standard is to follow up within 24 hours after the request has been received. Failing to return a call implies the caller is not important. This could cost your business a customer and potential sales.

Receiving Telephone Calls

As an employee, you will receive calls from colleagues and customers. Try to pick up the telephone on the first or second ring. It is important to identify yourself when you answer the phone. The protocol for answering a phone call varies from company to company, but you might say the name of the company first and then your own name. For example, your greeting may be, "Good afternoon, Horton and Associates, Celeste Burrell speaking."

After the caller identifies himself or herself, use the person's name during the course of the conversation. This helps make a personal connection with the caller and can also help you remember the person's name.

If you are working in customer service, you will receive training on how to interact with customers. Most businesses have a script to follow if you are receiving phone calls from a customer. The script can guide you in conducting a productive conversation and help you to follow the expected company protocol. However, remember the old adage, "the customer is always right." A customer who calls to complain should not be answered with an excuse or argument. Empathy should be demonstrated and an apology made to the customer for the inconvenience. Then ways to resolve the issue should be explored.

It will be necessary to record a voice mail greeting for those times when you cannot answer a call. Your voice mail greeting might be the first impression the caller will have of you and the business. This first impression will set the tone for all future conversations.

When recording your voice mail greeting, speak clearly with a positive, pleasant attitude. Your employer will likely have guidelines for recording the greeting stored in your company voice mail. State the company name, your name, and a specific message that lets the caller know when he or she can expect a return call. If you will be out of the office for that business day, include your return date in the message. The caller should be aware that you are unable to return the call immediately in the event that the call needs immediate attention. If your position requires immediate assistance for a customer, indicate the person and contact information for who the customer should call in your absence.

Placing Telephone Calls

As an employee, you will make calls on behalf of the company. These calls can be to customers or other people with whom you will conduct business. When you place the call and the telephone is answered, identify yourself. State your name, job title, and company. If the person who answers the phone is the person with whom you need to speak, state the reason you are calling. If you need to ask to be connected to another individual, identify the name of that person and thank the person to whom you are talking for his or her assistance.

Placing telephone calls for business purposes is a common task for most employees. You can improve your effectiveness and the productivity of a telephone call by planning before placing it. Any time you have a number of issues to discuss, questions to ask, or items of information to provide, develop a list ahead of time. Written notes will help you clearly express yourself and stay organized. They will also help you remember everything you intend to cover during the call. The goal is to be friendly and achieve your purpose in an efficient amount of time. Guidelines for making telephone calls are shown in Figure 8-1.

Leaving Voice Mail Messages

The ability to use voice mail in a professional manner is a valuable skill. When leaving a voice mail, speak slowly and clearly. State your name, job title, company, and phone number. It is important to keep the message brief and specify when you will be available for the person to return your call. It can be helpful to the receiver if you conclude the message by repeating your name and phone number as a closing.

Figure 8-1 Telephone etiquette is using good manners when speaking on the telephone.

Making Telephone Calls

- Prepare notes to use for the call.
- If the call will be lengthy, make an appointment in advance.
- When the telephone is answered, state your name, job title, and company.
- Speak clearly and in a normal tone of voice.
- Avoid using the speaker unless other people are in the room with you.
- At the end of the call, summarize any important points or decisions.
- If follow-up action is required, summarize what each person will do and when.
- Thank the person you called for his or her time, information, or assistance.

Goodheart-Willcox Publisher

Before you place a call, think about what you will say if you reach the person's voice mail. Determine how much you need to explain about the purpose of the call. Also, plan what you will ask the person to do. If you want the call returned, specify a time you will be available. The guidelines in Figure 8-2 will help you prepare to leave a voice mail message.

Leading a Meeting

Meetings are the primary way people come together in an organized fashion to discuss topics and issues. Some meetings may be informal in which members meet for a short time to casually discuss a topic. Generally, these meetings do not have rigid protocol that must be followed. However, there are times when formal meetings are necessary and should be conducted in an organized manner following proper etiquette.

Parliamentary procedure is a process for holding meetings so that they are orderly and democratic. Applying the procedures dictated by *Robert's Rules of Order* is an effective way to conduct a formal meeting.

Formal meetings require an agenda and someone to officially lead the meeting. The agenda should be distributed prior to the meeting. Attendees are expected to read the agenda and be prepared before the meeting begins.

The leader should begin the meeting on time and end it on time. Likewise, everybody attending should be present and ready at the established start time. Everyone's time is valuable, and there is no fashionably late option in professional situations.

It is sometimes a challenge to keep attendees on topic and to stick with the agenda. If important items come up that are not on the agenda, a separate meeting should be organized in the future for those topics.

If necessary, the leader should review ground rules before the meeting starts. Examples of meeting rules are:

- Participants should only speak when they *have the floor*, which means they have been given a turn to speak.

- Phones should be turned off and never placed on the desk or table.

- Laptops should not be used for checking e-mail while the meeting is in progress.

If a meeting is planned to be lengthy, a break should be given every two hours. This helps keep the meeting orderly. Other guidelines for conducting an effective meeting are shown in Figure 8-3.

Figure 8-2 Following the guidelines in this chart will result in a professional voice mail message.

Leaving Voice Mail Messages

- Speak clearly and at a pace that can be easily understood.

- State your name, company, your position or department, and your telephone number.

- If your name is unfamiliar or difficult to understand, clearly spell it.

- Leave a brief message stating the purpose of the call and when you will be available to receive a return call.

- If your call is urgent, say when you need a response.

Goodheart-Willcox Publisher

Figure 8-3 The guidelines in this table can help a person conduct an effective meeting.

Guidelines for Effective Meetings		
Before the Meeting	**During the Meeting**	**After the Meeting**
• Identify meeting purpose	• Adhere to parliamentary procedure	• Review notes
• Select participants	• Follow the agenda	• Send meeting notes to participants
• Reserve room and time	• Lead conversation	
• Send meeting invitation	• Respect others' time	
• Prepare agenda	• End meeting on time	
• Send agenda to all participants		

Goodheart-Willcox Publisher

Some meetings may include a virtual component for participants not in the same location. These types of meetings are often called *remote meetings*. The same rules of conducting a meeting should be followed when remote attendees are invited.

However, there are some nuances that should be considered when off-site participants are included. When setting a date and time, it is necessary to know which time zone the remote attendees are in so that the meeting is held during reasonable hours. A call-in number or website URL will need to be provided to those individuals who are off-site. This information should be sent to the remote attendees as early as possible so they can test their equipment and be prepared before the meeting begins.

If using real-time video conferencing, such as Skype, a dependable Internet connection is necessary. Specific software and equipment will be required and should be installed and tested before the meeting begins. If a meeting is conducted using a web-seminar site, such as GoTo Meeting, similar guidelines apply.

When the meeting begins, the leader should request permission from the participants to put them on speaker. Next, the leader should acknowledge those calling or logging in and make introductions. If appropriate, individuals can introduce themselves if there are not too many people in attendance for personal responses.

For those who are attending remotely, it is *polite* to put the phone on mute until ready to contribute to the conversations. It is *impolite* to be multitasking when a meeting is in progress rather than paying attention to what is transpiring in the conversations.

SUMMARY

- **(LO 8-1) Demonstrate how to make introductions in a professional situation.**
  Proper etiquette should be followed when making introductions, including using formal and appropriate language in every situation. If a person is introducing himself or herself, then the person's full name and position should be mentioned. If introducing other people, it is customary to say each person's full name and information to help the two people make conversation. When introducing a speaker, information about the person should be requested in advance to develop the introduction.
- **(LO 8-2) Explain protocol for handling business telephone calls.**
  Telephone calls are an important part of communication in the workplace. When representing a business, proper telephone etiquette should be followed when placing a call, answering a call, or leaving voice messages.
- **(LO 8-3) Describe how to conduct a formal meeting.**
  When conducting a formal business meeting, parliamentary procedure should be observed to maintain order. An agenda should be established and distributed to attendees prior to the meeting, and the meeting should begin and end on time.

GLOSSARY TERMS

Visit the G-W Learning companion website at **www.g-wlearning.com/careereducation/** to review the following glossary terms.

introduction   parliamentary procedure

REVIEW

1. Demonstrate how to make introductions in a professional setting.

2. Explain proper protocol for introducing two people who have not previously met.

3. Describe how to prepare an introduction to be used for a speaker at a formal event.

4. Explain protocol for handling business telephone calls.

5. Describe how to conduct a formal meeting.

APPLICATION

1. Throughout your life, you have probably been introduced to more people than you can remember. Improper introductions, however, tend to linger in our memories. Recall a time you were introduced to someone by a person who did not use proper etiquette. Describe the event.

2. It is customary when giving a speech to introduce yourself, as well as provide some background as to who you are. Write a one-paragraph introduction for yourself that you would use if you were to make a speech at a professional organization to which you belong.

3. You have been invited to introduce the CEO of your company at a formal presentation to members of the community. You will step to the podium and make the introduction using a microphone. Explain how professional etiquette will influence how you make the introduction.

4. Write a script for the receptionist for your company or school to use when answering the phone that applies appropriate telephone etiquette. Practice reading the message aloud until it has an appropriate professional tone.

5. The voice mail greeting for your personal telephone should reflect your professional image. As an adult in a working environment, there is the potential that an important business call could arrive on your personal phone. An inappropriate voice mail message could send the wrong message to an important caller and cost you an employment or other business opportunity. Write a script you would use for creating your voice mail greeting.

6. We all spend a lot of time on the phone. If you are a part of a remote or conference call, it is sometimes necessary to use a speaker. Outside of a conference call, cite reasons that are appropriate to place or be placed on speaker during a phone call.

7. More than likely, you have called a business and received an automated message informing you that the call may be monitored or recorded. Explain why a business would announce the fact they were recording a call and the reasons a business would record a customer call.

8. Most people will lead a meeting at some point in their careers. Reflect on meetings you have attended. Identify the day of the week that you think is most effective for a meeting and the time of day that people are most attentive. List specific actions you can take as a leader to make sure the room is conducive to the purposes of the meeting.

9. Time is important to everyone, especially in the workplace. Recall a meeting in which you participated that was either a waste of time or poorly led. Describe what happened.

10. There may be an occasion when you will participate as a caller in a remote meeting. Make a list of actions the leader of the meeting could take to help prepare you before the event begins.

INTERNET ACTIVITY

Handshake Protocol. A handshake is an important soft skill that can make or break your career. You don't want to be a "bone crusher" or a "fish" when you shake someone's hand. Research the appropriate professional business handshake. Make a list of protocol that you can use the next time you are in a professional situation where a handshake is required.

SKILLS PRACTICE

Visit the G-W Learning companion website at **www.g-wlearning.com/careereducation/** to access and complete the following soft skills practice activities:

Activity SS8-1 Introductions. Proper protocol should be used when introducing coworkers, managers, or customers to each other. Open the SS8-2 file, and describe the protocol for making introductions

Activity SS8-2 Parliamentary Procedure. Conducting a meeting is an important skill for the workplace. Open the SS8-1 file, and assess your knowledge of parliamentary procedure terms and phrases.

Listening Skills

baranq/Shutterstock.com

BEFORE YOU READ

Visit the G-W Learning companion website to view a video about soft skills. The video is available at **www.g-wlearning.com/careereducation/**

LEARNING OUTCOMES

On completion of this chapter, prepare to:

9-1   Explain the listening process.

9-2   Define purposeful listening.

9-3   Describe how to prepare to listen in a formal meeting.

Listening Process

Many people take listening for granted. However, there is no question that listening is a critical soft skill for career success. Routine business situations require that you listen carefully and evaluate what you hear. Actively listening to a supervisor or client can make the difference between successful and unsuccessful performance at work.

Hearing is the physical process of sound waves reaching a person's ears, which send signals to his or her brain. **Listening** is an intellectual process that combines hearing with evaluating. Just because you can hear a person speak does not mean you are listening to what is said. When you *listen*, you make an effort to process what you *hear*. To process what you hear, it is necessary to understand why the person is speaking, relate what you already know, and show attention. Effective listening is achieved by using the *listening process*. The listening process consists of the following steps, shown in Figure 9-1.

- *Receive.* Stop talking, focus on the sender, and hear the message.
- *Decode.* Assign meaning to words and sounds so the message can be understood.
- *Remember.* Take time to remember what is being said so the information can be used.
- *Evaluate.* Apply critical thinking skills to evaluate what was said.
- *Respond.* Give feedback to show the message was received.

Listening is an intellectual process that combines hearing with evaluating.

oneinchpunch/Shutterstock.com

Types of Listening

Following the steps in the listening process can improve your listening skills. There are two types of listening: passive listening and active listening.

Passive listening is casually listening to someone talk. You may or may not hear everything that is said, and you are not actively trying to understand. When you watch a movie, you are a passive listener. Passive listening is appropriate when you do not need to interact with the person speaking. Passive listeners are more interested in *hearing* and less interested in *listening*.

Active listening is fully participating as you process what a person says. It is used to get information, respond to requests, receive instructions, and evaluate persuasive speech. Active listeners consider the purpose of what is being said and show attention through body language and words. They know when to take notes, follow directions, comment, or remain quiet. Active listening is a required soft skill in the workplace.

Figure 9-1 Effective listening is achieved by using the listening process.

Goodheart-Willcox Publisher

There are several types of active listening, as shown in Figure 9-2. Each type serves a specific purpose. You may engage in more than one type of active listening at a time.

Show You are Listening

When someone is speaking, it is necessary to show attention. The following are some key ways to show you are listening:

- Face the speaker and give your full attention.

- Let the person finish speaking before you contribute to the conversation.

- Engage in eye contact to signal that you are focused. Avoid staring, which can be intimidating and distracting.

- Lean toward the speaker to indicate you are paying attention.

- Be appropriately responsive. Smile or laugh at a joke and frown at bad news.

- Nod your head when you understand a point. If you are puzzled by something, let the speaker know by furrowing your brow or asking a question.

Be mindful that the speaker will be evaluating your body language. Nonverbal cues, such as roving eyes and inappropriate facial expressions, can communicate indifference and may even be considered rude.

Listen with Purpose

When you speak, you have a purpose or reason for delivering the message. Likewise, when you listen, you are listening to someone who has a purpose or reason for delivering the message. Your job as a listener starts by recognizing the purpose of the person speaking. It is necessary to concentrate on what the speaker is saying, and if necessary, take notes on what is being said.

Your purpose for listening varies depending on whether you are listening in a one-on-one conversation, in a group discussion, or as a member of a large audience.

Figure 9-2 Active listening is fully participating as you process what a person says.

Types of Active Listening	
Appreciative listening	Appreciative listening is the process of listening for enjoyment. Listening to music is an example of appreciative listening.
Critical listening	Critical listening occurs when specific information or instructions are needed. For example, a computer technician must use critical listening to determine a customer's problems and needs.
Deliberative listening	Deliberative listening is the process of determining the quality or validity of what is being said. For example, if a salesperson tells you that by purchasing a piece of equipment you will save thousands of dollars each year, you must evaluate this statement to determine if it is valid.
Empathetic listening	Empathetic listening occurs when the listener attempts to put himself or herself in the speaker's place and understand how he or she feels. Customer service representatives often use empathetic listening to understand why a customer is upset. By understanding the issue, the customer service representative may be better able to assist the customer.
Reflective listening	Reflective listening occurs when the listener demonstrates an understanding of the message by restating what was said. The listener does not try to change the meaning of the message, but may paraphrase to show understanding. All active listening involves reflective listening.

Goodheart-Willcox Publisher

You will be a more effective listener if you can identify your purpose and adapt your listening behavior accordingly.

The purpose for listening varies depending on the type of conversation.

Rido/Shutterstock.com

Listen for Specific Information

If you must listen for a great deal of data, prepare in advance whenever possible, and find out as much as you can about the topic. Having this prior knowledge will give you something to which you can relate your new knowledge. Before you go to a meeting, attend a conference, or make a telephone call, decide what information you hope to gain. Bring a catalog, report, budget, or any materials that will be discussed.

When someone is responding to your question or request for specific information, listen carefully. In some cases, a response can be very long, or the person may use language that is not clear. Make sure you understand all parts of the response and its details. Ask questions to clarify any points that are confusing.

Listen to Instructions

When others are instructing you, help them out by actively listening to what they are saying. If you are meeting with an individual or in a group where directions are being given, ask questions and make comments to clarify and confirm the information discussed. If necessary, politely ask the person who is speaking to slow down or repeat a point. As you listen, try to anticipate your future needs. Will you need additional information after the meeting? Find out when and where you can get help if a problem should arise and make note of it.

When possible, give feedback to the speaker to show you understand the information that is being presented. Sometimes, simply making eye contact tells the person you are listening. If there is an opportunity to give comments or ask questions, do so. Your feedback will be appreciated by the person delivering the information.

Make sure you have all of the information before leaving the meeting, and write a brief summary of the information you learned. *Summarizing* is an active listening technique that can help to ensure you remember the important information. When you summarize, you write or think through all of the main points you just heard.

Listen to Requests

Requests come in all shapes and sizes. Some are simple and need only a brief response. Others can be tedious and time-consuming. In many cases, your first decision must be whether you can or should accomplish whatever is being asked. Your second decision may be whether you can do so in the allotted time. When you receive a request, consider the following:

- Determine whether the request is one of your assigned job tasks.
- Listen to be sure you understand the request.
- Ask follow-up questions to clarify complex issues.
- Make comments that summarize what you are to do.
- Avoid relying on your memory. Take notes, especially for numbers, dates, and other details.

Listen to Persuasive Talk

When someone is trying to persuade you, that person has a purpose: to influence your attitude or behavior. When you know what he or she wants, you will be better able to analyze what is being said. When you recognize persuasive talk, determine the purpose of being persuaded by asking yourself the following questions:

- What does the speaker have to gain?

- Whom does he or she represent?

- What does he or she want me to do or believe?

- What are the pros and cons of this issue?

When a person is trying to persuade you, he or she attempts to predict your objections and argue against them in advance. Avoid the mistake of being a passive listener. Recognize that effective persuasive talk is carefully prepared and is adjusted to obtain the desired results. As a listener, you should prepare to analyze incoming information. Take into consideration the purpose of the persuasive talk as well as your own needs and motivations.

Case Study

Listening

Everett Collection/Shutterstock.com

In 1995, J.K. Rowling had finished writing her first manuscript for *Harry Potter and the Philosopher's Stone* and was looking for a publisher. Her literary agent contacted Nigel Newton, chairman of Bloomsbury Publishing, and gave him a sample of the work. Newton then gave the sample to his 8-year-old daughter, who was part of the book's target market. She read it and immediately requested more of the unpublished text. On a hunch, Newton listened to the enthusiastic feedback of his small literary critic and purchased the publishing rights to Rowling's story. The Harry Potter series went on to become the best-selling book series of all time and has been translated into 73 different languages. Had Nigel Newton not listened to his 8-year-old daughter, he may have been another in the line of publishers that rejected J.K. Rowling, and her story may never have been told. This historic publishing event demonstrates the importance of listening regardless of the speaker's status, age, or experience.

1. What type of listening did Nigel Newton apply?

2. Was it professional for Newton to give his 8-year-old daughter Rowling's manuscript?

3. What kinds of communication skills do you think Newton's daughter used to convince him to publish the novel?

4. What do you think prompted Newton to listen to his daughter?

Formal Meetings

Formal situations require extra listening effort. Interviewing for a job, meeting with a manager, and sharing a business lunch with clients are situations that require special attention. You must be prepared and ready to interact with the other parties involved. This interaction will include listening, as well as sharing information verbally.

However, if you are attending a formal presentation, your primary purpose is to listen and pay attention. You can prepare to listen by arriving early, sitting in the front, taking notes, fighting barriers, and providing feedback.

Arrive Early

Arriving early is not merely a courtesy to the speaker and other meeting participants, but it is also an aid to your listening. By arriving early, you have time to settle in, familiarize yourself with your surroundings, and greet people you know.

The beginning and end of any speaking event are often crucial. Speakers typically introduce and summarize main points both at the beginning and the end. By missing the first few minutes of a presentation, you cannot benefit from the speaker's attempt to focus the discussion and introduce main ideas. Arriving late is disruptive and disrespectful to others in the audience.

Sit in the Front

The front of the room usually provides fewer distractions. You are less likely to be disturbed by the people sitting between you and the speaker. From the front, you can hear the speaker better and see any visuals presented with less effort. By sitting in the front of the room, you will be able to participate more easily in the listening process.

Take Notes

Effective note-taking requires careful, active listening. Write down the speaker's points that are meaningful to your purpose for listening. You must not only hear what is said, but also comprehend, evaluate, and translate or summarize the information. Then, determine if the information is important enough to write down. If it is, you must quickly record it. Continue listening unless the speaker stops while you write. Remember that note-taking is not a substitute for active listening. Suggestions for taking efficient notes are shown in Figure 9-3.

Figure 9-3 Taking notes is one way to demonstrate active listening.

Taking Good Notes

- Be selective. Write down only what is important or what you may not remember.

- Organize your notes as you write, if possible. Let the format of your notes correspond to the speaker's message.

- Use abbreviations and symbols. If the notes are for you only, cut as many corners as you like as long as the notes remain useful.

- Avoid noting information that appears in a handout. Highlight or put a check mark in the margin of the handout to remind yourself of key points.

- Write down the main point of a visual aid. If it contains data you need later, write down the source or ask the speaker afterward for a copy of the visual.

- Often speakers summarize the most important points in the closing. This is a good time to be listening carefully with pen ready, if necessary.

Goodheart-Willcox Publisher

It is important to write down the things you must do following a discussion or meeting. Relying on memory is not a good idea. Carefully listen for any instructions, whether directly stated or implied, and write them down. You will often leave meetings with many things on your mind, some of which you will forget if you do not take notes.

Fight Barriers

Good listeners fight external distractions and barriers so they can give all of their attention to the task of listening. Be aware of the barriers, both internal and external, that might interfere with good listening. Concentration helps to keep internal distractions, which are created by one's own mind, in check. There are several strategies to fight barriers to listening.

- *Be attentive*. Attentive listeners become involved in what the speaker is saying. Inattentive listeners become distracted because they are bored or are multitasking. Turn off your digital devices. Follow along with the speaker. Resist the temptation to daydream.

- *Be flexible*. Flexible listeners are open to new ideas. Inflexible listeners refuse to listen to a speaker who has said or implied something they disagree with. They tune out the speaker and are not interested in learning.

- *Be unbiased*. Unbiased listeners do not make judgments. Being biased interferes with your ability to listen. Choose not to decide in advance whether or not a speaker is credible or deserves your attention.

- *Be empathetic*. To *empathize* with the speaker is to put yourself in his or her shoes. Imagine how you would feel as the speaker.

Provide Feedback

When possible, provide feedback to the speaker by asking questions and making comments. Be aware that the tone of questions and comments can influence the communication process. *Friendly questions* that ask for clarification or further information are usually welcomed by a person making a presentation. Such feedback puts the speaker at ease and provides an opportunity to repeat or elaborate on a point. By asking questions and making comments that do not mean to belittle or invalidate the speaker, you show that you are listening and interested. You also demonstrate that you have enough confidence in the speaker to seek more information. Figure 9-4 shows examples of friendly questions.

If spoken in an unfriendly tone, questions and comments can put a speaker on the defensive and create communication barriers, as shown in Figure 9-5. Challenging questions or comments are not a form of constructive feedback. Even if the speaker has a good response to an unfriendly question or comment, the challenge may create an uncomfortable atmosphere.

Figure 9-4 Asking appropriate questions is a way to provide feedback and demonstrate interest.

Friendly Questions

These questions can be considered friendly questions. Friendly questions are usually welcomed by the speaker.

- Did your marketing questionnaire elicit any information on family income?
- This summary sheet says the year's sales goal is 10 percent higher than last year's. Is that 10 percent over last year's actual sales or 10 percent over budgeted sales?
- How expensive is this new technology for fuel conservation?
- I agree we must get our budget back on track, but do we have some specific ways to get around the higher prices in the marketplace?
- If we give them a copy of the appendix, will it answer all of their questions?

Goodheart-Willcox Publisher

Figure 9-5 Unfriendly questions can put a speaker on the defensive and create communication barriers.

> ## Unfriendly Questions
>
> These questions may be considered unfriendly questions. Unfriendly questions can put up a barrier between you and the speaker.
>
> - Last week you said last month's sales were up 10 percent, but today you say they were down five percent. Which is it?
> - You claim there are no problems with clear-cutting forests, but how do you account for the article in last week's *Forestry Magazine*, which listed several problems with clear-cutting?
> - That sounds like a very high number. Do you have empirical evidence to support that claim?
> - You always talk about participative management, but have you really implemented it in this department?

Goodheart-Willcox Publisher

Avoid the pitfalls of being unfriendly by carefully phrasing your question or comment. Consider the following points when providing feedback:

- Ask questions at the appropriate time.
- Be sure the question is relevant.
- Limit the length of your question.
- Observe good diplomacy.
- Refrain from criticizing.
- Never get personal.

It is rude to interrupt a speaker in a group meeting or a presentation. Instead, write down questions or comments and wait until the speaker invites them. A presenter may welcome questions during a presentation or indicate that questions and comments will be taken at the end. If you have more than one question or comment, pause between them to give others a chance to participate.

Questions should not be asked, nor comments made, that do not relate to the topic. The speaker may not be able to answer, and other listeners will probably become impatient. If you need to discuss an unrelated topic, approach the speaker after the formal session concludes.

When appropriate to ask questions and make comments, they should be kept short. It is inappropriate to get into a long, one-on-one discussion. This is inconsiderate to the group. If you need to pursue a discussion beyond a follow-up question or comment, do so after the formal session.

No matter how much you disagree, always maintain a professional tone. If you ask a good question or make a good comment in an unprofessional manner, your lack of professionalism is what people will remember. If the speaker appears to have given incorrect information, give the speaker the benefit of the doubt and carefully phrase your question or comment.

Small details should never become distractions. Sometimes a speaker makes a general point with which you agree, but supports it with a detail with which you disagree. Do not challenge the detail unless you foresee it being misused later. In most cases, the general point is the more important aspect and the rest can be disregarded.

If a speaker says something with which you disagree on principle or that you find offensive, consider letting it go. As a listener, it is not your role to challenge a speaker on behalf of your beliefs. If your disagreement is intense, approach the speaker in private. However, your goal should be to share a different perspective with the speaker, not to embarrass or to argue with him or her.

SUMMARY

- **(LO 9-1) Explain the listening process.**
  Hearing is a physical process, while listening involves evaluating what you hear. The steps of the listening process are receive, decode, remember, evaluate, and respond. Listening can be passive or active.
- **(LO 9-2) Define purposeful listening.**
  When someone is speaking, he or she is doing so for a reason. Therefore, the job of the listener is to recognize the reason for the message and listen with a purpose. The purpose for listening varies depending on the type of message and size of the audience. Listening behaviors must be adapted to fit the venue, purpose, and type of speech.
- **(LO 9-3) Describe how to prepare to listen in a formal meeting.**
  A listener can show that he or she is listening during a formal meeting in many ways. Arriving early, sitting in the front, taking notes, fighting barriers, and providing feedback demonstrate to the speaker that a listener is engaged.

GLOSSARY TERMS

Visit the G-W Learning companion website at **www.g-wlearning.com/careereducation/** to review the following glossary terms.

active listening

hearing

listening

passive listening

REVIEW

1. List the steps of the listening process.

2. Differentiate between passive listening and active listening.

3. How can a person demonstrate that he or she is listening to the speaker?

4. Define purposeful listening.

5. List ways a person can demonstrate listening in a formal meeting.

APPLICATION

1. Identify a person with whom you are in regular contact and consider to be a good listener. What does that person do to make you think he or she is listening to you?

2. Identify a person with whom you are in regular contact and consider to be a poor listener. What does that person do to make you think he or she is not listening to you?

3. Recall the listening strategies you used as your instructor presented this information. List the actions you took that demonstrated you were actively listening.

4. When a person is speaking, he or she expects that the people hearing the message will also be listening. It is considered rude to ignore someone who is speaking. How can poor listening skills affect a person's professional image?

5. Reflect on your listening skills. Describe the routine you use when listening to a lecture to make sure you pay attention.

6. Identify strategies that you use for note-taking during a conversation with another person or in a presentation.

7. Describe strategies you use to fight barriers when listening to a lecture.

8. Often, listening barriers are the biggest obstacle to communication. Consider a time when you created a listening barrier. What was the result?

9. Describe a situation in which you had a conversation with a person and used empathetic listening. Explain words or phrases you used to express empathy.

10. Recall a time when you asked a question of a speaker during a presentation. Was it friendly or unfriendly? Describe the effect of your question on the speaker and presentation.

INTERNET ACTIVITY

Active vs. Passive Listening. Using the Internet, watch videos of two different speeches. For the first speech, practice passive listening. For the second speech, practice active listening. The next day, write down as much detail as you can recall from each speech. Which one could you better recall? Write several paragraphs explaining what you did to practice active listening and how those actions aided in your recall.

SKILLS PRACTICE

Visit the G-W Learning companion website at **www.g-wlearning.com/careereducation/** to access and complete the following soft skills practice activities:

Activity SS9-1 Listening Skills. Listening is an important soft skill that can help a person be effective in his or her career. Open the SS9-1 file, and rate your personal listening skills.

Activity SS9-2 Listening Types. There are five types of active listening. Open the SS9-2 file, and evaluate your skill level for each type.

CHAPTER 10

Written Communication

wavebreakmedia/Shutterstock.com

BEFORE YOU READ

Visit the G-W Learning companion website to view a video about soft skills. The video is available at **www.g-wlearning.com/careereducation/**

LEARNING OUTCOMES

On completion of this chapter, prepare to:

10-1 Describe writing etiquette.

10-2 Explain the importance of social media etiquette.

Writing etiquette is the art of using good manners when communicating in written form.

SpeedKingz/Shutterstock.com

Writing Etiquette

Writing etiquette is the art of using good manners when communicating in written form. It involves careful selection of language and tone, as discussed in Chapter 6. Your professional image is at stake each time you write a letter, send an e-mail, or post a comment or video on a social media site.

Writing etiquette involves deciding when it is appropriate to send a letter or e-mail. It also includes writing thank-you notes and responding to RSVPs.

Letters

Business letters are used as a medium to communicate with individuals or businesses outside of the organization when formal communication is more appropriate than e-mail. A letter is written to:

- make a request;
- respond to a request;
- inform or provide information;
- persuade or convince the receiver to take an action; or
- instruct or provide direction or guidance.

Standard English and appropriate language should be used for business letters. A professional tone should be applied and business etiquette followed. Business letters are printed on letterhead stationery and include the following standard letter elements:

- *Date*. Month, day, and year the letter is being written.
- *Inside address*. Name, title, and address of the recipient.
- *Salutation*. Greeting that identifies recipient and always begins with Dear.
- *Body*. Message of the letter that consists of the introductory paragraph, message, and closing paragraph.
- *Complimentary close*. Sign-off for the letter.
- *Signature*. Writer's name and title.
- *Notations*. Initials of the person who keyed the letter and reference to enclosures.

It is important to note that etiquette dictates a letter be addressed to a specific person unless it is intentionally directed to an organization. It may take a phone call or Internet search to get the correct name, but it is worth the effort to personalize a message. The receiver's name should be spelled correctly and the appropriate title used, such as *Dr.*, *Mr.*, or *Ms.* The title *Mrs.* is rarely used in business writing. Titles such as *Professor* and *Reverend* should be spelled in full rather than abbreviated. If you are unsure of a person's gender, the person's full name should be used.

If you need to write a letter without the name of a specific person, avoid traditional greetings, such as *Dear Sir* or *Gentlemen*. You may use *Ladies and Gentlemen*; however, the best course is to use words that describe the role of the person such as *Dear Customer* or *Dear Editor*.

There are two standardized letter formats: block and modified block. A **block style letter** is formatted so all lines are flush with the left margin. No indentations are used. Figure 10-1 shows a letter formatted in the block style.

A **modified block style letter** places the date, complimentary close, and signature to the right of the center point of the letter. All other elements of the letter are flush with the left margin. Figure 10-2 shows a letter formatted in the modified block style.

Figure 10-1 The block style letter is formatted so all lines are flush with the left margin.

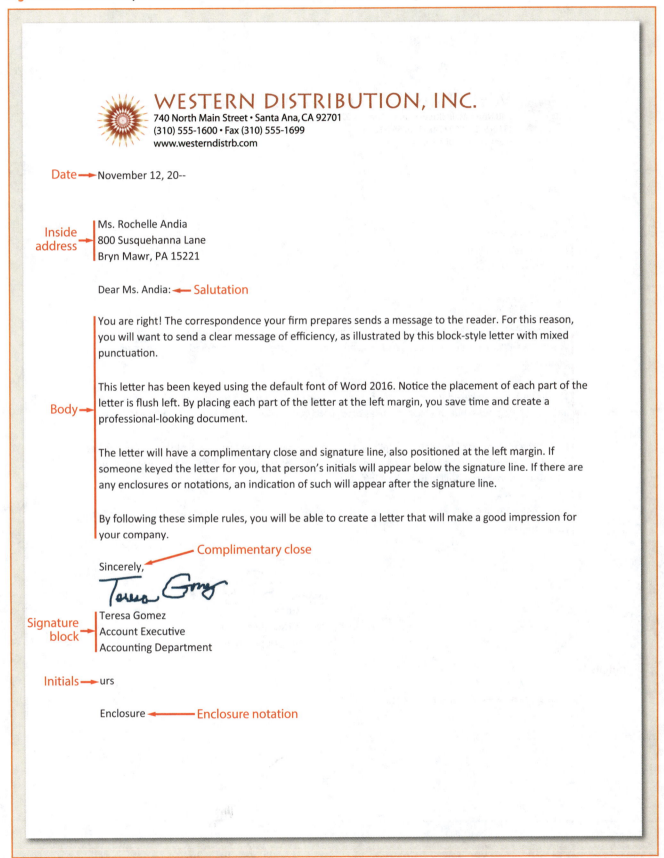

Figure 10-2 The modified block style letter places the date, complimentary close, and signature to the right of the center point of the letter.

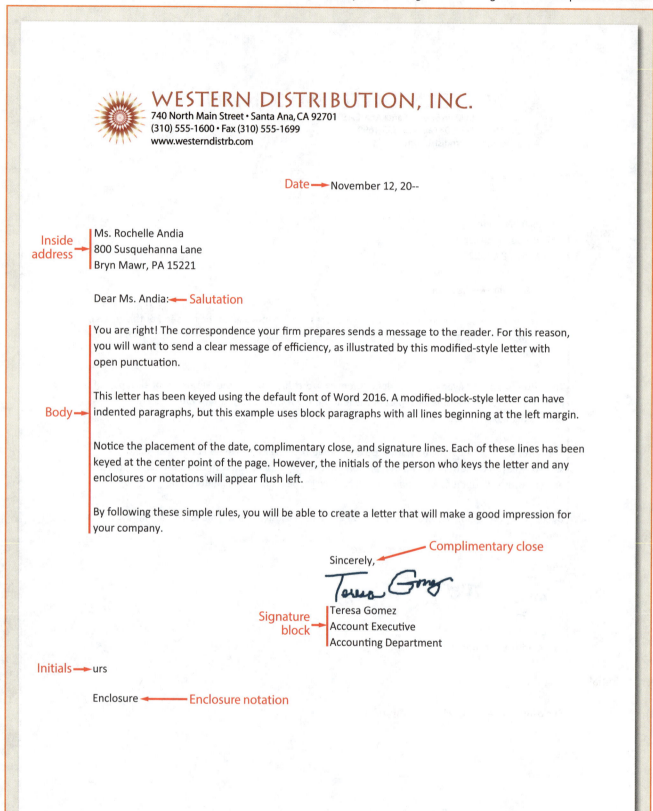

E-Mail

E-mail is considered an acceptable form of business communication if a formal letter is not required. An appropriately formatted e-mail is shown in Figure 10-3. When sending e-mail as a representative of your business, use Standard English and run the spell-check feature before sending. Remember, you are in a professional environment, and your e-mail could be forwarded to others who might make judgments about what you have written.

The primary recipients should be placed in the **TO:** line. These are the people who you expect to respond. Those who you do not expect to respond should be listed in the **COPY:** line, abbreviated as *Cc:*. The **BLIND COPY:** line, abbreviated as *Bcc:*, is used to list people whose names and e-mail addresses will not be visible to all others receiving the e-mail. For an e-mail sent to a large number of people, it is courteous to use the blind copy function to ensure the e-mail addresses of the recipients remain private.

The subject line should be limited to one concise topic. For example, a subject of *Hello* is not suitable for business communication, but *August Business Report* may be appropriate. Each word should start with a capital letter in accordance with the rules of capitalization.

When responding to an e-mail, select the **Reply** button so the e-mail trail is intact. This helps the reader keep track of the details of the conversation. However, if there is a need to respond and bring up a new topic after reading an e-mail, send a new e-mail and note the topic in the subject line. Creating a new e-mail with a new subject line makes it easier to keep the flow of information understandable and managed.

Figure 10-3 A properly formatted e-mail follows netiquette and reinforces the sender's professionalism.

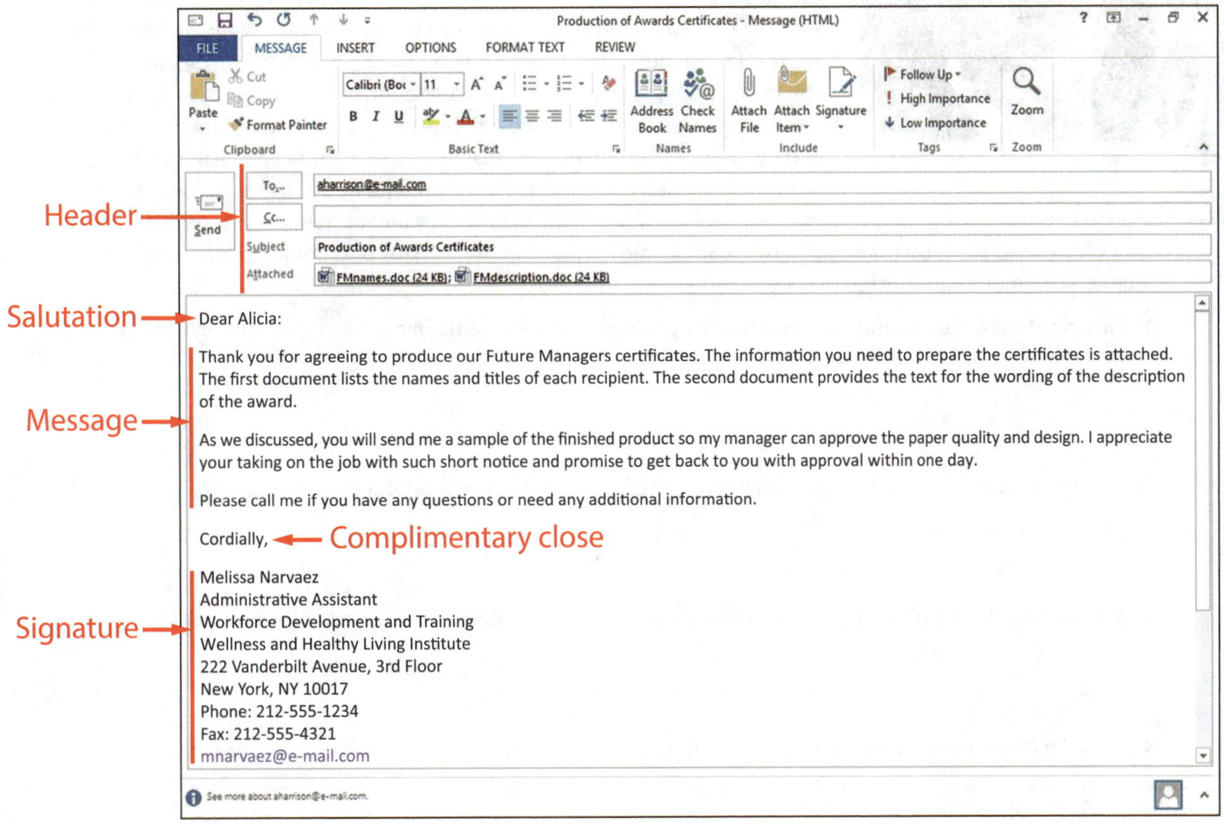

Goodheart-Willcox Publisher

In most businesses and organizations, people address each other by their first names in e-mails. The salutation *Dear* may be used as in a letter, depending on whether it is a formal or informal e-mail. Netiquette should be used when writing the body of the message, and a courteous thank-you at the end of the body is usually appropriate for business correspondence. For a formal e-mail, it is standard to include your full name and contact information at the bottom of the message for the convenience of the reader.

Care should be taken when sending attachments to ensure the recipient's inbox can handle the size and type of file sent. It is a common courtesy to notify the recipient that you will be sending an attachment in a follow-up e-mail. Unless an e-mail with an attachment is expected, it is standard practice for many businesses to delete it without reading to avoid computer viruses.

It is important to respond promptly to e-mails. A delay in an e-mail response can affect the company's image, making it seem as though the company is uninterested or uncaring about the subject matter. When you are planning to be out of the office, the automated reply feature should be used to send a message stating when you will return. An example of an appropriate message is, "Thank you for your e-mail. I am out of the office until Tuesday, at which time I will respond to your message." This is a professional courtesy. It allows the sender to know you are unavailable, rather than being careless about responding.

Case Study

National Archives

Thank-You Note

In 1994, shortly after being diagnosed with Alzheimer's, former President Ronald Reagan wrote an open (i.e., not private) thank-you letter to the people of the United States of America. In it, he wrote about his diagnosis and decision to make it known publicly with the hopes of raising awareness. In perhaps one of the most humbling gestures by a US president, he closed the letter by thanking the American public for electing him president and allowing him the honor of serving as such. Despite the fact that he had been out of office for five years at the time of the letter, it will be forever remembered as a gracious way to close the Reagan presidency. Most presidents and public officials thank their constituents when getting elected, but few have ever penned an actual thank-you letter to their voters. This example perhaps best demonstrates the power and sentimentality that a handwritten thank-you carries.

1. Describe how the emotional response to a handwritten thank-you letter differs from the emotional response to one that is keyed via word-processing software, printed, and mailed.

2. In what ways did President Reagan's thank-you letter serve as a lesson on etiquette to the country?

3. Explain how this act of writing a thank-you note demonstrated humility on the part of the President.

4. How did President Reagan's thank-you letter influence US citizens' perception of his professional image?

Thank-You Notes

It is good manners to write thank-you notes when someone does something special for you. A thank-you may be in the form of a printed letter sent through the mail or an e-mail. Handwritten notes are more personal, but a well-written e-mail is sufficient in most cases.

A thank-you note should be written within a week of the courtesy. The person should be thanked for taking the time to do what they did. Any important points of the act should be repeated, and a strong appreciation of what was done should be reinforced.

RSVP

RSVP is an initialism for the French expression *répondez s'il vous plaît*, which means *please respond*. When you receive an invitation that says RSVP, the sender is asking you to respond to either accept or decline. It is rude not to respond to an invitation. You should reply whether or not you will attend the function.

The invitation may indicate if a guest is welcome. If that is the case, note if you will be attending alone or with a guest. If bringing a guest, this is often referred to as *plus one*.

It is good manners to write thank-you notes when someone does something special for you.

StockLite/Shutterstock.com

Social Media Etiquette

Social media includes websites and apps that allow individual users to network online by creating and sharing content with one another. For many individuals, businesses, and governments, social media is an important part of everyday life. It is a useful tool to help build a personal brand, develop a community, and communicate with others.

It is easy to take communicating in real time for granted and to write whatever you are thinking. As you know, once the words are recorded, they cannot be taken back. For that reason, the writing process should be followed and thoughtful consideration should be given before anything is posted. Inappropriate language, photos, or comments are never acceptable.

If you are representing your business on social media, professional etiquette is required. Most organizations have guidelines for posting information about the company. Proper writing, grammar, and general rules of appropriateness are expected to be followed. It is important to take digital communication responsibilities seriously.

If you are representing yourself on professional social media sites, careful consideration should be given to what is posted. Professional sites, such as LinkedIn, can be useful to an individual for networking and career opportunities. Etiquette and ethics dictate that information about personal education and work experience is honest and accurate. Remember that what is published on the page will be read by current and future employers.

Writing for personal social media can be challenging. Your family and friends want all your activities and photos to be posted for their enjoyment. However, posting too much personal information can be detrimental to your career and can be seen by professional contacts. These sites must be taken seriously and used with caution. Anything posted on the Internet creates a digital footprint. You have heard this many times—online communication will never really go away. It can, and will, follow you in your personal and professional life.

SUMMARY

- **(LO 10-1) Describe writing etiquette.**
  Writing etiquette is the art of using good manners when communicating in written form. It involves careful selection of language and tone. Writing etiquette involves deciding when it is appropriate to send written communication, including letters, e-mails, thank-you notes, and event RSVPs.
- **(LO 10-2) Explain the importance of social media etiquette.**
  Developing social media etiquette is equally as important as a person's writing ability. Items posted to social media accounts live forever in a digital footprint and can affect a person's ability to get or maintain employment. Inappropriate language, photos, or comments are never acceptable, especially when representing a business.

GLOSSARY TERMS

Visit the G-W Learning companion website at **www.g-wlearning.com/careereducation/** to review the following glossary terms.

block style letter   modified block style letter

REVIEW

1. Describe writing etiquette.

2. Identify the elements of a business letter.

3. Describe the format of a block style letter.

4. Describe the format of a modified block style letter.

5. Explain the importance of social media etiquette.

APPLICATION

1. Writing etiquette is a reflection of a person's personal and professional image. Summarize what you would tell a student or your child about the importance of writing etiquette.

2. Professional communication includes both letters and e-mail. Identify criteria that you would use to decide when a business message should be written in letter format or be sent via e-mail.

3. Explain how writing a letter, sending an e-mail, or posting a comment or video on a social media site as a representative of your company can impact the reputation of the business.

4. E-mail is effective when used properly but is sometimes overused in the workplace. Employees often send an e-mail instead of walking down the hall to talk to someone. Discuss the reasons for using or not using e-mail to communicate in the workplace.

5. Explain the potential consequences of responding to a work-related e-mail and hitting the "reply to all" option.

6. In what types of situations is a handwritten thank-you more appropriate than one that is keyed via word-processing software, printed, and mailed?

7. You have received a small gift from your supervisor as an expression of gratitude for working late to meet a deadline. Draft a thank-you note to your supervisor. Would you write the note by hand, on the computer and print it, or send an e-mail? Explain your choice of communication.

8. Not responding to an RSVP is not only rude, but it can be an inconvenience to the person hosting an event. If an invitee doesn't respond to an invitation and shows up at an event, what impact can this have on the host?

9. Assume you are in charge of the Facebook page for your company. You hurriedly wrote a post in response to a customer question. An hour later, a customer responded to your post and commented that there were errors in the message. How would you handle this situation?

10. Personal social media accounts can be viewed by anyone on the Internet, including potential employers. Review your own personal accounts. Identify any posts that would reflect negatively on your professional image.

INTERNET ACTIVITY

Writing a Negative Message. There will be times in your professional career when you are tasked with delivering a negative message in the form of written communication. A letter with a negative message will be read differently than one with a positive message. Conduct an Internet search using the phrase *writing a negative message*. Note some of the ways a negative message can be conveyed in an appropriate, businesslike manner.

SKILLS PRACTICE

Visit the G-W Learning companion website at **www.g-wlearning.com/careereducation/** to access and complete the following soft skills practice activities:

Activity SS10-1: Letter Formatting. Proper formatting of business letters is necessary for professional communication. Open the SS10-1 file, and format the letter in the style of your choice.

Activity SS10-2 Editing Skills. Review your editing skills. Open SS10-2, and follow the directions to improve the structure of the content in the document.

Writing and Interviewing for Employment

Racorn/Shutterstock.com

BEFORE YOU READ

Visit the G-W Learning companion website to view a video about soft skills. The video is available at **www.g-wlearning.com/careereducation/**

LEARNING OUTCOMES

On completion of this chapter, prepare to:

11-1 Describe a résumé, cover message, and portfolio.

11-2 Explain how to apply for a job online and in person.

11-3 Discuss the process of preparing for a job interview.

11-4 Define post-interview protocol.

11-5 Describe the hiring process.

The process of applying for employment typically involves completing a job application.

DW labs Incorporated/Shutterstock.com

Résumé, Cover Message, and Portfolio

When seeking employment, it will be necessary to create a résumé and cover message. Some job applications may also require a career portfolio. Each document should be professionally written and formatted.

Résumé

A **résumé** is a document that profiles a person's career goals, education, and work history. Its purpose is to prove to a potential employer that person's experiences and skills match the qualifications of the job. Think of a résumé as a snapshot that tells the employer who you are and why you would be an asset as an employee.

The first impression most employers will have of you is your résumé. It is a reflection of your professional image, so it should be well written, error free, and fit on one page, as shown in Figure 11-1. A simple format should be used with top and bottom margins approximately one inch. Side margins should also be one inch but can be adjusted as needed to fit the résumé on one page. Font selection should be conservative and professional, such as Calibri 11 pt. or Times New Roman 12 pt. Decorative fonts are distracting and should never be used on a résumé. A typical résumé is organized into the following sections:

- contact information
- objective
- education
- work experience
- memberships and professional affiliations
- community service experience
- honors, awards, and publications

A section should only be included if you have relevant information to list. For example, if you do not belong to a professional organization, do not use this heading.

The job description for which you are applying may note specific hard skills, as well as soft skills, that the employer is requesting. The *education* section is a good place to list relevant skills that highlight your qualifications for the job.

When saving a résumé, use your name and the word *résumé* in the filename. For example, if you are Pat Accura, your filename would be PatAccuraResume. This helps the employer identify to whom the résumé belongs.

Cover Message

A **cover message** is a letter or e-mail sent with a résumé to introduce the applicant and summarize his or her reasons for applying for a job. It is a sales message written to persuade the reader to grant an interview. A cover message provides an opportunity to focus a potential employer's attention on the individual's background, important soft skills and hard skills required for the position, and work experience that matches the job the person is seeking.

Writing a cover message is an important part of applying for a job. It sets the tone for the résumé that follows. A cover message should focus on your qualifications without being boastful, while expressing why you are a good fit for the company. It should not repeat details found in the résumé. Rather, it should highlight your key qualifications that are specific to the job for which you are applying. The message should also explain how you heard about the position.

A cover message, like all professional communication, must be completely error free. Whether it is a printed letter or an e-mail message, standard letter formatting should be followed. Figure 11-2 shows an example of a cover message that will be printed and mailed. Figure 11-3 shows an example of a cover message that will be sent by e-mail.

Figure 11-1 A résumé is a document that profiles a person's career goals, education, and work history.

Latisha Turgess

518 Burnett Road, Randallstown, MD 21123

(555) 555–1234

lturgess@e-mail.com

www.linkedin.com/in/latishaturgess

Objective: To use my technical skills as a robotics and automation specialist in the manufacturing industry and further develop my skills as a professional.

Education: Associate degree, June, 2017, Essex Community College, Baltimore, MD
Major: Engineering Technology, Robotics & Automation Specialization

Relevant Courses:

Programming Logic & Design	Robotics & Automation I
Electrical Studies I & II	Manufacturing Processes
CADD/Computer Modeling	Fluid Power

Relevant Skills:

Solid Works and CADD	Cloud Cap Piccollo
C# Programming Language	Stitching Sonar and Data Graphics
Photoshop and Illustrator	Microsoft Office Specialist Certification
Electronics and Automation	

Work Experience: August, 2016 to present
CNC Machinist, McHenry Manufacturing, Baltimore, MD
Assist in job setup and operation of CNC equipment, perform tooling maintenance, and ensure that all required processes are completed to produce parts that meet quality and ISO standards

January, 2013 to August, 2016
Sales associate, Wal-Mart, Randallstown, MD
Provide customer service in electronics department

Community Service: January, 2014 to present
Volunteer, Habitat for Humanity, Baltimore, MD
Assist in building houses

Honors: Dean's list four years

Figure 11-2 A cover message is a letter or e-mail sent with a résumé to introduce the applicant and summarize his or her reasons for applying for a job.

39 Lucas Lane
Jasper, TN 37347
June 5, 20--

Ms. Cheryl Lynn Sebastian
Director of Administration
Jefferson City Convention & Visitors Bureau, Inc.
100 E. High Street
Jefferson City, MO 65101

Dear Ms. Sebastian:

The position you advertised in the *Network Journal* on March 14 for a customer service trainee is exactly the kind of job I am seeking. According to your ad, this position requires good business communication skills. As you can see by my résumé, my educational background and experience working at a travel agency prepared me for this position.

For the past two years, I worked as a part-time receptionist at the Barcelona Travel Agency. While working there, I gained experience dealing with customers on the telephone, as well as greeting walk-in customers and handling their requests for information. I also had the opportunity to observe the full-time staff at work and attend department meetings. At these meetings, I learned the importance of satisfying customer needs and meeting the challenges of working with the general public.

As the enclosed résumé shows, I will graduate from the University of Missouri in early June. While in college, I took several business courses, including a business communication class. These classes helped me develop good English and verbal communication skills. In addition to my education and work experience, I can offer your organization a strong work ethic and the ability to fluently speak Spanish.

I would like very much to meet you and hope that you will contact me by phone or e-mail to schedule an interview for the position. If I do not hear from you within the next couple of weeks, I hope you will not mind if I follow up with a phone call.

Sincerely yours,

Pat Accura

Pat Accura

Enclosure

Figure 11-3 A cover message can be sent in an e-mail when applying online. Notice that the applicant's résumé is attached to the e-mail.

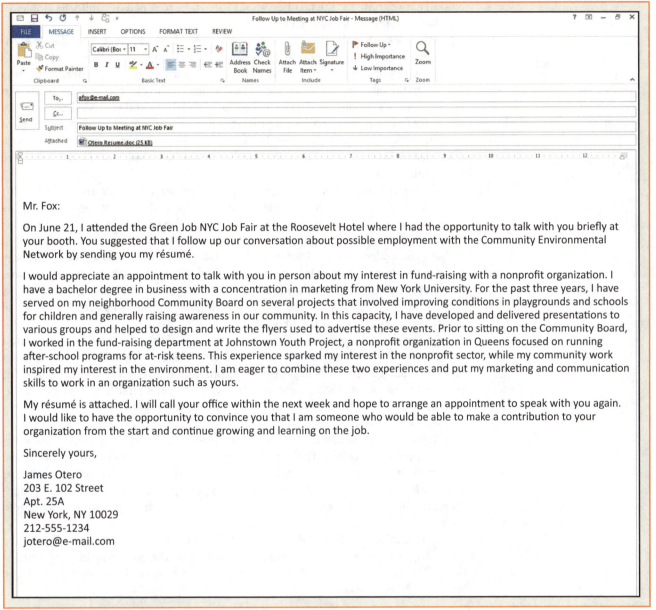

Portfolio

When applying for a job, it will be necessary to tell the employer why you are qualified for the position. To support your qualifications, you may need to create a portfolio. A **portfolio** is a selection of related materials that are collected and organized to show the qualifications, skills, and talents that support an individual's career or personal goals. Artists and communication professionals are typically expected to present portfolios of their creative work when seeking jobs or admission to educational institutions. However, portfolios are used in many professions to demonstrate an applicant's credentials.

There are some common elements generally included in a portfolio such as photocopies of certificates of accomplishment, diplomas, and professional licenses.

Samples of work, letters of recommendation, and any documents that show a talent or skill appropriate for the position should also be a part of a portfolio. Examples of additional items are shown in Figure 11-4.

Résumés generally do not include references but may be included as a separate document in a portfolio. A **reference** is a person who knows an applicant's skills, talents, or personal traits and is willing to recommend him or her. References will probably be someone from your professional network. These individuals can be someone for whom you have worked or with whom you provided community service. However, you should not list relatives as references. References, like a résumé, should be updated throughout a professional career. A person who was a reference for you when you were in college may not be an appropriate reference five years into your career.

Consider which references can best recommend you for the position for which you are applying. Always get permission from the person before using his or her name as a reference, and notify the person the companies and positions for which you are applying.

As you collect material for your portfolio, you will need an effective strategy to keep the items clean, safe, and organized for assembly at the appropriate time. Structure and organization are important when working on an ongoing project that includes multiple pieces. A large manila envelope works well to store hard copies of documents, photos, awards, and other items.

There are multiple ways to prepare a portfolio for presentation. The method you choose should allow the viewer to easily navigate and find items. The simplest approach is to print and organize your portfolio material in a binder. Or, you could create an electronic presentation with slides that have links to documents, videos, graphics, or sound files. Another option is to place the files on a CD or USB flash drive.

Websites are another method for presenting a digital portfolio. A personal website can be created to host the files with a main page and links to various sections. Each section page could have links to pages with documents, videos, graphics, or sound files. Alternatively, LinkedIn can be a good place to house portfolio documents. If you place your material on a site owned by a company, read the user agreement for rules of use.

A portfolio is a living document and should be updated regularly. Before going to an interview, it is a good idea to review the material in your portfolio and make sure it is up-to-date. In addition, it may need customizing for the specific job interview.

Figure 11-4 A portfolio is a selection of related materials that are collected and organized to show the qualifications, skills, and talents to support an individual's career or personal goal.

Examples of Portfolio Elements

- diploma
- continuing-education certificates
- professional licenses
- letter of introduction
- letters of recommendation
- military record and awards
- references
- résumé
- SAT, ACT, or GRE scores
- transcripts
- videos (presentations or other talents)
- writing samples

Goodheart-Willcox Publisher

Application Process

The process of applying for employment typically involves completing a job application form along with submitting a résumé and cover message. Some job employment opportunities may also require the submission of a portfolio.

In today's market, the job application process is typically completed online. However, there are some employers who utilize the traditional process of an applicant physically visiting the human resources department and applying in person.

Before applying for a position, confirm the application process described in the job advertisement. A call to the company's human resources department can also help clarify what is expected by the employer.

Case Study

IB Photography/Shutterstock.com

Résumé Fraud

In January 2012, Yahoo! hired Scott Thompson as their new CEO. His résumé listed impressive experience, including work at PayPal and a subsidiary of Visa Inc., as well as bachelor degrees in accounting and computer science from Stonehill College in Massachusetts.

In April 2012, a Yahoo! investor publicly questioned Thompson's academic credentials. He was accused of padding his résumé with the addition of a computer science degree. Stonehill College confirmed that he earned only a bachelor degree in accounting. At that point, Thompson stated that the executive placement firm with which he was a client must have added the computer-science degree to his résumé without his knowledge. The executive placement firm quickly produced documentation proving it was not involved in the fraud. In May 2012, Yahoo! released a statement announcing that Thompson was no longer with the company.

In addition to the public humiliation and tarnished reputation, lying on his résumé put Thompson at risk of trouble with the law. His fraudulent credentials were listed on Yahoo!'s annual report that is filed with the US Security and Exchange Commission. CEOs are required to personally certify that the company's SEC filings are accurate. This lie is likely to follow Scott Thompson for the remainder of his career.

1. What impact does the act of committing résumé fraud have on Thompson's integrity?

2. Name and describe a self-management skill that Thompson seemed to be lacking when he chose to falsify his résumé?

3. Do you think Thompson was being arrogant or overconfident thinking that he wouldn't be exposed when he falsified his résumé? Support your opinion.

4. How does this incident impact Scott Thompson's professional image?

Applying Online

The first step in the online application process may be to complete a job application. A *job application* is an employment form that requests contact information, education, and work experience. Even though much of this information may be repeated on your résumé, many companies require an official job application to be completed.

Next, you may be required to upload a résumé, copy and paste information into a form on the site, or send it as an e-mail attachment. Be aware that copying and pasting text into a form usually strips out formatting such as tabs, indentations, and bold type. Avoid pasting text that is formatted in any way. Even if the formatting is retained, it can make the information difficult to read when the employer accesses the application. You may need to adjust the layout of your résumé after uploading it or pasting it into an online application form.

Carefully review each document before clicking the **Submit** button. Applying online does not mean you can ignore proper spelling, grammar, and usage. Your application materials will be the employer's first impression of you. Submitting an application with misspellings or other errors may persuade an employer to eliminate you as a serious candidate.

There may be an opportunity to include a cover message and portfolio with the application. Follow the directions on the website for attaching additional employment materials.

Applying in Person

The traditional way of applying for employment is to visit the human resources office of the company to which you are applying. When you arrive, be prepared to complete a job application. Write neatly and use only blue or black ink. Carefully review the form before submitting it. Like a résumé or cover message, a job application needs to be free of spelling, grammar, and usage errors.

Bring with you a copy of your résumé, cover message, and portfolio. All documents should be on the same high-quality, white or off-white paper and printed using a laser printer. Do not fold or staple the documents. Instead, use a large envelope, file folder, or paper clip to keep the pages together. If using an envelope or folder, print your name on the outside and list the components included.

Preparing for an Interview

If your résumé and cover letter have passed the employer's screening process, you may be invited to interview. A first interview may be conducted either over the telephone or in person.

To prepare for a job interview, learn as much as you can about the position as well as the company. People in your professional network may be able to help you find information about the position or company.

Much information can be obtained from the company's website, which will likely have an *About Us* section. This section of the website may include press releases, annual reports, and information on the company's products or services. You may also consider calling the human resources department for additional information. The human resources department often has materials specifically developed for potential employees. When you call the company, use your best telephone etiquette while speaking with the person who answers the phone. Introduce yourself, state your purpose for calling, and be prepared with a list of questions to ask. Be polite and say "please" and "thank you" when speaking with each person so that you make a positive impression.

While preparing for an interview, it is important to be mentally prepared in the event that a performance test is required as part of the interviewing process. For example, a graphic artist may be asked to create a simple design using the software the company uses as a production tool. This will test not only the person's design abilities, but also his or her ability to use the software. Be prepared to take a performance test, if requested.

Interview Questions

Interview questions are intended to assess an applicant's skills and abilities and to explore an individual's personality. Answers to these questions will help determine whether a candidate will fit in with the company team and the manager's leadership style. Interviewers also want to assess an individual's critical-thinking skills by asking him or her to cite specific examples of completed projects or problems he or she solved. During the interview, the applicant's communication skills will also be observed.

Before an interview, try to anticipate questions the interviewer is likely to ask and write down your answers.

kataijudit/Shutterstock.com

Common Questions

Before the interview, try to anticipate questions the interviewer is likely to ask you. The following are some common interview questions.

- What are your strengths?
- What are your weaknesses?
- What about this position interests you?
- What do you plan to be doing five years from now?
- Why do you want to work for this organization?

Write down your answers to these questions. Practice answering the questions while in front of a mirror. An important part of the communication process is nonverbal communication—body language is especially important. Practicing in front of a mirror allows you to see your nonverbal communication.

Another way to prepare for an interview is to conduct a mock interview with a friend or instructor. A **mock interview** is a practice interview conducted with another person. Practice until you can respond with your planned responses naturally and without reading them. The more prepared you are, the more relaxed, organized, competent, and professional you will appear to the interviewer.

Hypothetical Questions

Interviewers may also ask hypothetical questions. **Hypothetical questions** require a candidate to imagine a situation and describe how he or she would act. Frequent topics of hypothetical questions relate to working with and getting along with coworkers. For example, "How would you handle a disagreement with a coworker?" You cannot prepare specific answers to these questions, so you need to rely on your ability to think on your feet.

For these types of questions, the interviewer is aware that you are being put on the spot. In addition to what you say, he or she considers other aspects of your answer as well. Body language is first and foremost. Avoid fidgeting and looking at the ceiling while thinking of your answer. Instead, look at the interviewer and calmly take a moment to compose your thoughts. Keep your answer brief. If your answer runs on too long, you risk losing your train of thought. Try to relate the question to something that is familiar to you and answer honestly.

Do not try to figure out what the interviewer wants you to say. Showing that you can remain poised and project confidence carries a lot of weight, even if your answer is not ideal. In many cases, the interviewer is not as interested in *what* your response is as much as *how* you responded. Was your response quick and thoughtful? Did you ramble? Did you stare blankly at the interviewer before responding?

Behavioral Questions

Interviewers may ask behavioral questions. **Behavioral questions** are questions that draw on an individual's previous experiences and decisions. Your answers to these types of questions indicate past behavior, which may be used to predict future behavior and success in a position. The following are some examples of behavioral questions.

- Tell me about a time when you needed to assume a leadership position in a group. What were the challenges, and how did you help the group meet its goals?
- Describe a situation where you needed to be creative in order to help a client with a problem.
- Describe a situation when you made a mistake. How did you correct the mistake and what measures did you put in place to ensure it did not happen a second time?

Again, you cannot prepare specific answers to these questions. Remain poised, answer honestly, and keep your answers focused on the question. Making direct eye contact with the interviewer can project a positive impression.

Questions an Employer Should Not Ask

State and federal laws prohibit employers from asking questions on certain topics. It is important to know these topics so you can be prepared if such a question comes up during an interview. It is illegal for employers to ask questions about a job candidate's religion, national origin, gender, or disability. Questions about age can only be asked if a minimum age is required by law for a job. The following are some examples of questions an employer is not permitted to ask a candidate.

- What is your religion?
- Are you married?
- What is your nationality?
- Are you disabled?
- Do you have children?
- How much do you weigh?

If you are presented with similar questions during the interview, remain professional. You are not obligated to provide an answer. You could respond, "Please explain how that relates to the job." Or you could completely avoid the question by saying, "I would rather not answer personal questions."

Questions to Ask the Employer

Keep in mind that the questions you ask, and how you ask them, reveal details about your personality. In the early stages of the interview process, your questions should demonstrate that you would be a valuable employee and are interested in learning about the company. The following are some questions you may want to ask.

- What are the specific duties of this position?
- What is company policy or criteria for employee promotions?
- Do you have a policy for providing on-the-job training?
- When do you expect to make your hiring decision?
- What is the anticipated start date?

Some questions are not appropriate until after you have been offered the job. Questions related to pay and benefits, such as vacation time, should not be asked in the interview unless the employer brings them up. Sometimes, however, an interviewer may ask for your salary expectations. If you prefer not to answer at the time of the interview, you can simply tell the interviewer that the salary is negotiable.

Dress for an Interview

A face-to-face interview is typically the first time a potential employee is seen by a company representative. First impressions are important, so professional dress is critical. When dressing for an interview, consider what you wish your professional image to portray. Figure 11-5 illustrates typical attire worn for a job interview.

The easiest rule to follow is to dress in a way that shows you understand the work environment and know the appropriate attire. Interviewing apparel should be somewhat more formal than is called for in the work environment. For example, if the work environment is business-casual dress, a business-professional outfit with a jacket would be appropriate at the interview. If the work environment requires a uniform, business-casual dress might be appropriate for the interview.

It is better to dress conservatively than in trendy clothing. Employers expect interviewees to present their best image in appearance, as well as skills and qualifications. Dressing more conservatively than needed is not likely to be viewed as a disadvantage. However, dressing too casually, too trendy, or wearing inappropriate clothing is likely to cost you the job. Additionally, personal expressions, such as visible tattoos or piercings, may be seen as inappropriate for the workplace by the employer.

Figure 11-5 Appropriate dress for an interview is a display of professionalism.

Appropriate Attire for a Job Interview

Women
- Wear a suit or dress with a conservative length.
- Choose solid colors over prints or flowers.
- Wear pumps with a moderate heel or flats.
- Keep any jewelry small.
- Have a well-groomed hairstyle.
- Use little makeup.
- Avoid perfume or apply it very lightly.
- Nails should be manicured and of moderate length without decals.
- Cover all tattoos.

Men
- Wear a conservative suit of a solid color.
- Wear a long-sleeved shirt, either white or a light color.
- Tie should be a solid color or a conservative print.
- Wear loafers or lace-up shoes with dark socks.
- Avoid wearing jewelry.
- Have a well-groomed haircut.
- Avoid cologne.
- Nails should be neatly trimmed.
- Cover all tattoos.

Daxiao Productions/Shutterstock.com; AlexandreNunes/Shutterstock.com; Goodheart-Willcox Publisher

After the Interview

Shaking hands and leaving the building does not mark the end of the job-interview process. After the interview has ended, it is important to send a thank-you message to the person, or persons, with whom you met. It is equally important to evaluate the experience. Performing these actions will ensure that you not only stay on the radar of the company, but improve your skills before your next interview as well.

Thank-You Message

Immediately after an interview, and no later than 24 to 48 hours, a *thank-you message* should be written to the interviewer. It may be in the form of a printed letter sent through the mail or an e-mail. Remind the person, or persons, of your name and reiterate your enthusiasm, but do not be pushy. Extend your appreciation for his or her time. An example of a thank-you message is shown in Figure 11-6.

Interview Evaluation

Evaluate your performance as soon as you can after the interview. Asking yourself the following questions can help in evaluating your performance.

- Was I adequately prepared with knowledge about the company and the position?
- Did I remember to bring copies of my résumé, list of references, portfolio, and any other requested documents to the interview?
- Was I on time for the interview?
- Did I talk too much or too little?
- Did I honestly and completely answer the interviewer's questions?
- Did I dress appropriately?
- Did I display nervous behavior, such as fidgeting, or forget things I wanted to say?
- Did I come across as composed and confident?
- Which questions could I have handled better?

Every job interview is an opportunity to practice. If you discover that you are not interested in the job, do not feel as though your time was wasted. Make a list of the things you feel you did correctly and things you would do differently next time.

Figure 11-6 A thank-you message should remind the interviewer of the applicant's name and reiterate enthusiasm for the position without being pushy.

Dear Ms. Cary:

Thank you for the opportunity to discuss the position of associate fashion designer.

I am very excited about the possibility of working for Clothing Design Specialists. The job is exactly the sort of challenging opportunity I had hoped to find. I believe my educational background and internship experience will enable me to make a contribution, while also learning and growing on the job.

Please contact me if you need any additional information. I look forward to hearing from you.

Sincerely,

Hiring Process

A successful interviewing process may lead to a job offer with the company for which an applicant has applied to work. Most companies make a job offer contingent on employment verification, reference checks, background checks, and credit checks. In addition, the applicant may be required to submit to drug testing. If the applicant passes the screenings, the job offer is generally made official, employment forms are completed, and the new employee starts his or her job.

Employee Checks

Employment verification is a process through which the information provided on an applicant's résumé is checked to verify that it is correct. Former employers typically verify only the dates of employment, position title, and other objective data of employees who are no longer at the company. Most employers will not provide opinions about employees, such as whether or not he or she was considered a good worker. Reference checks are also made at this time.

Another important part of the employment process is a background check. A **background check** is an investigation into personal data about a job applicant. This information is available from governmental records and other sources. The employer should inform you that a background check will be conducted. The company must ask for written permission before obtaining the background check report. A person is not legally obligated to give permission, but an employer can reject a candidate based on insufficient or unverified background information.

When granted permission by a job applicant, an employer may perform a credit check on that person. A credit report reflects a person's credit history, which some employers use as an indicator of a person's level of responsibility. There is no solid evidence that credit history will indicate an applicant's performance, but it is a common screening device. Many states have regulations on how credit reports can be used and employers may not be able to run this check.

In states where permitted, companies may require drug and alcohol screenings of job applicants. These screenings are commonly performed at a sterile, off-site location, such as a lab, and may be blood, urine, saliva, or other medical tests. A failed drug or alcohol test can result in not being offered a job.

In addition to governmental sources, many employers use Internet search engines, such as Google, to search for information on candidates. Employers may also check social networking websites, such as Facebook and Twitter. Be aware of this before posting any personal information or photos. These checks might work to your advantage or against you, depending on what the employer finds. It is up to you to ensure that the image you project on social networking sites is not embarrassing or, worse, preventing you from achieving your career goals.

Employment Forms

After the job applicant is successful in the hiring process and is offered the job, a considerable amount of time will be spent in the human resources department completing necessary forms for employment. Common employment forms include Form I-9, Form W-4, and benefit forms. Come prepared with the personal information required to complete a multitude of forms. You will need your Social Security number, contact information for emergencies, and other personal information.

Form I-9

A **Form I-9 Employment Eligibility Verification** is used to verify an employee's identity and that he or she is authorized to work in the United States. This form is from the US Citizen and Immigration Services, a governmental agency within the

US Department of Homeland Security. Both citizens and noncitizens are required to complete this form. An example of a Form I-9 is shown in Figure 11-7.

The Form I-9 must be signed in the presence of an authorized representative of the human resources department. Documentation of identity must be presented at the time the form is signed. Acceptable documentation commonly used includes a valid driver's license, a state-issued photo ID, or a passport.

Form W-4

A *Form W-4 Employee's Withholding Allowance Certificate* is used by the employer to determine the appropriate amount of taxes to withhold from an employee's paycheck. Deductions are based on marital status and the number of dependents claimed, including the employee. The amounts withheld are forwarded to the appropriate governmental agency.

At the end of the year, the employer sends the employee a *Form W-2 Wage and Tax Statement* to use when filing income tax returns. This form summarizes all wages and deductions for the year for an individual employee.

Benefits Forms

The human resources department will provide a variety of forms that are specific to the compensation package offered by the employer. These forms may include health insurance, life insurance, corporate membership, or profit-sharing enrollment forms. Be prepared to complete multiple forms on your first day.

Figure 11-7 A *Form I-9 Employment Eligibility Verification* is used to verify an employee's identity and that he or she is authorized to work in the United States.

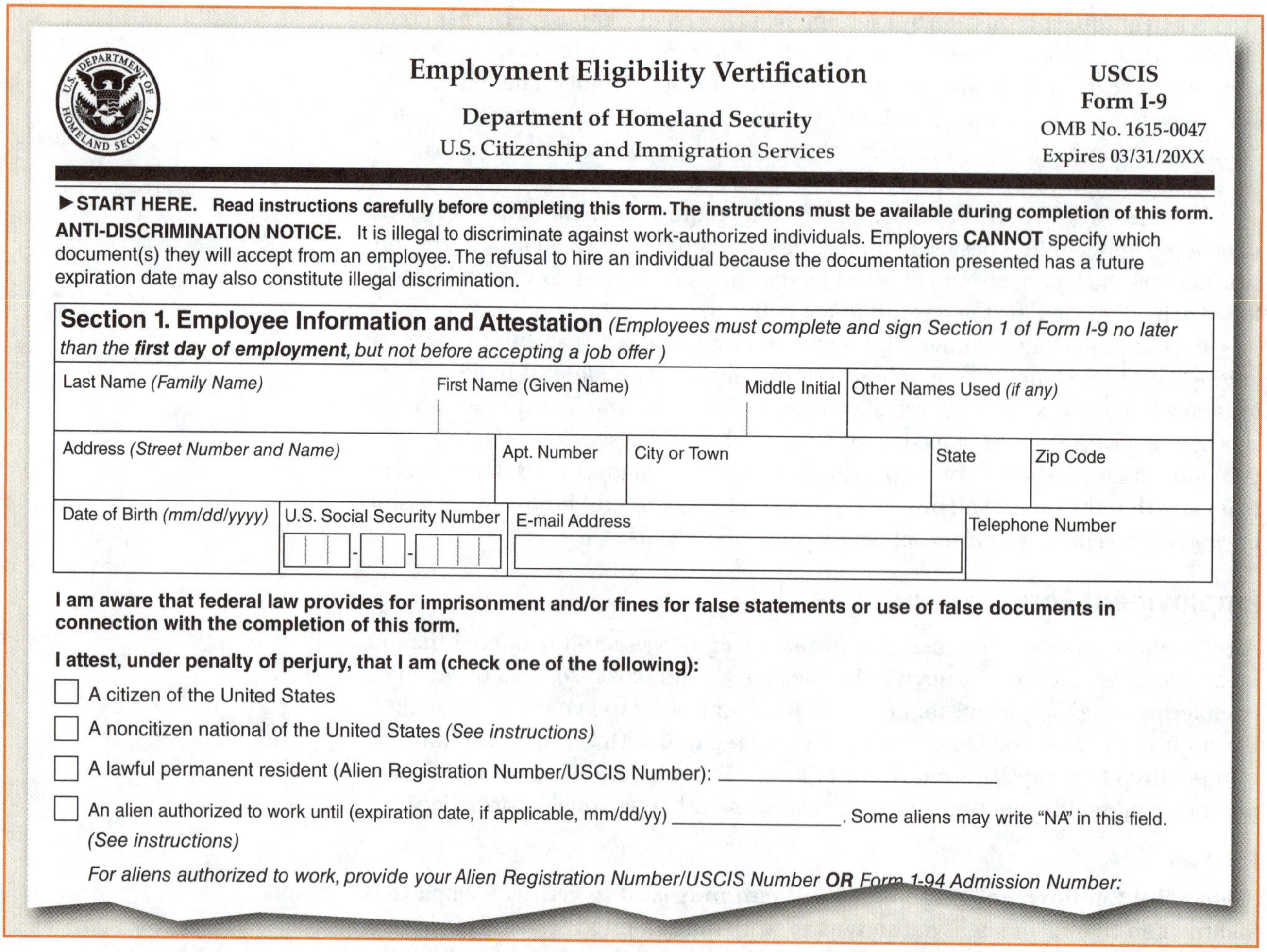

Employment Eligibility Verification

Department of Homeland Security

U.S. Citizenship and Immigration Services

USCIS
Form I-9
OMB No. 1615-0047
Expires 03/31/20XX

▶**START HERE. Read instructions carefully before completing this form. The instructions must be available during completion of this form.**

ANTI-DISCRIMINATION NOTICE. It is illegal to discriminate against work-authorized individuals. Employers **CANNOT** specify which document(s) they will accept from an employee. The refusal to hire an individual because the documentation presented has a future expiration date may also constitute illegal discrimination.

Section 1. Employee Information and Attestation *(Employees must complete and sign Section 1 of Form I-9 no later than the* ***first day of employment****, but not before accepting a job offer)*

Last Name *(Family Name)*	First Name (Given Name)	Middle Initial	Other Names Used *(if any)*

Address *(Street Number and Name)*	Apt. Number	City or Town	State	Zip Code

Date of Birth *(mm/dd/yyyy)*	U.S. Social Security Number	E-mail Address	Telephone Number
	- -		

I am aware that federal law provides for imprisonment and/or fines for false statements or use of false documents in connection with the completion of this form.

I attest, under penalty of perjury, that I am (check one of the following):

☐ A citizen of the United States

☐ A noncitizen national of the United States *(See instructions)*

☐ A lawful permanent resident (Alien Registration Number/USCIS Number): ______________

☐ An alien authorized to work until (expiration date, if applicable, mm/dd/yy) ____________. Some aliens may write "NA" in this field. *(See instructions)*

For aliens authorized to work, provide your Alien Registration Number/USCIS Number **OR** *Form I-94 Admission Number:*

Source: US Department of Homeland Security; Goodheart-Willcox Publisher

SUMMARY

- **(LO 11-1) Describe a résumé, cover message, and portfolio.**
  A résumé is a document that provides potential employers with a profile of a person's career goals, work history, and job qualifications. A cover message typically accompanies a résumé. Its purpose is to provide an introduction to the job applicant and explain why he or she is the right person for the position. In addition to a résumé and cover message, a portfolio may be submitted. A portfolio is a selection of related materials that are collected and organized to show the qualifications, skills, and talents to support an individual's career or personal goals.

- **(LO 11-2) Explain how to apply for a job online and in person.**
  Most applicants apply for a position online. This includes the completion and submission of an online job application and uploading of a résumé, cover message, and potentially a portfolio. The traditional way to apply for a job is to visit the human resources department of a company and complete a job application in person and submit the application documents in print form.

- **(LO 11-3) Discuss the process of preparing for a job interview.**
  To prepare for a job interview, an applicant should learn as much about the employer and position as possible. It is also helpful to make a list of questions to ask the interviewer and practice answers to common interview questions. Conducting a mock interview with a friend or instructor is a good way to prepare for the actual interview. When choosing what to wear, select an outfit that demonstrates an understanding of the company dress code.

- **(LO 11-4) Define post-interview protocol.**
  After an interview has concluded, it is important to send a thank-you message to the interviewer. The thank-you message can be handwritten or sent via e-mail. Next, the interview process should be evaluated. Evaluating the interview is the best way for an applicant to practice and sharpen his or her interviewing skills.

- **(LO 11-5) Describe the hiring process.**
  Most companies make a job offer contingent on employment verification, reference checks, background checks, and credit checks. In addition, the applicant may be required to submit to drug testing. If the applicant passes the screenings, the job offer is generally made official, employment forms are completed, and the new employee starts his or her job.

GLOSSARY TERMS

Visit the G-W Learning companion website at **www.g-wlearning.com/careereducation/** to review the following glossary terms.

background check	hypothetical questions
behavioral questions	mock interview
cover message	portfolio
employment verification	reference
Form I-9 Employment Eligibility Verification	résumé

REVIEW

1. Describe a résumé, cover message, and portfolio.

2. Explain how to apply for a job online and in person.

3. Discuss the process of preparing for a job interview.

4. Describe post-interview protocol.

5. Describe the hiring process.

APPLICATION

1. A résumé should be kept to one page, if possible. This requires that the information you record is focused and important to the job for which you are applying. The education section is an opportunity to showcase your soft skills as well as hard skills. Make a list of the skills you would list on your résumé that you think are important for a potential employer to note.

2. Create a list of documents you would include in your career portfolio. If you already have a portfolio, provide an inventory of the items you currently have.

3. References are typically submitted as a separate document. Make a list of people in your network who you would request permission of to use as a reference.

4. Some companies require an applicant to take a personality assessment, such as the Myers-Briggs Type Indicator, as part of the job application process. Discuss your opinion as to why you think an employer would require such a test.

5. Write an answer for each of the following potential interview questions.
    A. What makes you a good employee?

    B. What are your strengths?

    C. What are your weaknesses?

6. Create a list of five questions you might ask during the interview. Be aware of how you word questions to make the best impression on the interviewer.

7. Before going to an interview, you should try on your clothing and accessories the day before the interview. Why is this important?

8. Write several paragraphs that you would include in a thank-you letter to a potential employer who interviewed you for a position.

9. You have recently been interviewed for the position of assistant manager at a local restaurant. Write a follow-up letter after you have been informed that another candidate was hired.

10. Reflect on your last job application experience. Summarize what you did well during the application process, and evaluate the areas in which you did not perform so well.

INTERNET ACTIVITY

Dressing for an Interview. There are many articles that offer advice on dressing for an interview. Visit a site such as Monster.com and read the professional advice offered for interview attire.

Personality Assessment. Some companies require applicants to take a personality assessment as part of the application process. One well-known instrument is the Myers-Briggs Type Indicator (MBTI). Visit the MBTI website and learn about the assessment and what it measures.

Onboarding. Onboarding is a term used to describe the processes through which new employees obtain knowledge and skills to become effective members of the organization. Conduct an Internet search for the term *onboarding* and learn what you can do to make the process successful on your next job.

SKILLS PRACTICE

Visit the G-W Learning companion website at **www.g-wlearning.com/careereducation/** to access and complete the following soft skills practice activities:

Activity SS11-1: Résumé Writing. Proper creation and formatting of a résumé is a reflection of the professional image of the applicant. Open the SS11-1 file, and format the résumé. When you have finished, create your own personal résumé.

Activity SS11-2: Cover Message Writing. When applying for employment, a cover message is written to accompany the résumé. Open the SS11-2 file, and write a cover message for employment.

Activity SS11-3: Employment Application Form. Job applicants are generally required to complete an application form. Some of these forms can be completed online. Others require the applicant to handwrite the information. Open the SS11-3 file, and practice completing the form on the computer; then print and complete by hand in ink.

Activity SS11-4: Employment Forms. New employees are required to complete multiple forms for the employer. These will typically be handwritten in ink and should be done so with your best handwriting. Open the SS11-4 file, and practice completing employment forms.

CHAPTER 12 Teams

Production Perig/Shutterstock.com

BEFORE YOU READ

Visit the G-W Learning companion website to view a video about soft skills. The video is available at **www.g-wlearning.com/careereducation/**

LEARNING OUTCOMES

On completion of this chapter, prepare to:

12-1   Describe teams in the workplace.

12-2   List the steps of the conflict-resolution model.

12-3   Identify examples of behaviors exhibited by difficult people.

12-4   Describe leadership in the workplace.

A team is a group of two or more people who work together to achieve a common goal.

Rawpixel.com/Shutterstock.com

Teams in the Workplace

A **team** is a group of two or more people who work together to achieve a common goal. A high-performing team can tackle projects that are too big for one person to undertake or require various talents and skills to perform. The terms *team*, *department*, and *group* are sometimes used interchangeably.

Many businesses develop and organize their employees into functional teams. A *functional team* is brought together for a specific purpose. Members share the same skill set and expertise. They may not be able to perform each job required, but they understand the responsibilities of each team member. The group comes together as a unit to meet specific goals. This is common in organizations that have teams such as marketing, sales, and production. These are the basic work groups in most businesses. Each team has specific goals and responsibilities it must meet.

There are situations when a specific problem needs to be solved or a special project needs attention. In these situations, companies often create cross-functional teams. A *cross-functional team* is made up of representatives from various functional teams that come together to solve a specific problem or perform a task. A cross-functional team may be called a *task force* or *committee*. This type of team is beneficial for solving issues that affect the entire organization. Having representation from each functional team helps create a sense of ownership and interest in solving an issue for the common good. When the project is complete, the task force might disband.

Teamwork

Teamwork is the cooperative efforts by individual team members to achieve a goal. Members of a team take pride in what they do, share responsibilities and decision-making, and develop a sense of accomplishment when a project is completed. This happens only when the team members work together and focus on their assigned tasks. Being a *team player* is a soft skill that is important to career success. Effective team players contribute ideas and personal effort, share goals, and assume ownership for their actions. They fulfill their promises to teammates, support each other, and encourage success.

Each team member plays a role in the success of the group. For example, some individuals are encouragers who focus on team harmony and are always asking others for opinions. Task-oriented team members identify and define tasks and help see that they are accomplished. There are many different team member roles that contribute to success. Examples of member roles are shown in Figure 12-1.

Teamwork requires collaboration. *Collaboration* means working together to create a solution or address a challenge. **Collaboration skills** are behaviors that individuals exhibit when working with others to achieve a common goal and maintain working relationships. This includes sharing ideas and making compromises when the greater good of the team is at stake. To *compromise* is to give up an individual idea so that the group can come to a solution. Collaboration and compromise are two important skills necessary for effective teamwork.

Figure 12-1 Group members can take on one or more unique roles.

Group Member Roles		
compromiser	prioritizer	supporter
encourager	innovator	harmonizer
initiator	organizer	energizer
orienter	information seeker	gatekeeper

Goodheart-Willcox Publisher

Group Dynamics

Group dynamics are the interacting forces within a group or team, including the attitudes, behaviors, and personalities of all members. The dynamics of a team are the result of the attitudes of the members and how they interact with each other. Group dynamics can have a positive or negative influence on how a team reaches its goals.

The *group process* is how a team comes together to get things done. When a team is organized, it may not necessarily be immediately productive. Psychologist Bruce Tuckman described a group-development process, as shown in Figure 12-2, which includes the following four stages:

- *Forming.* The group comes together and starts to get to know each other.

- *Storming.* Members express their individual needs and opinions; conflict can develop at this stage.

- *Norming.* Collaboration and cooperation develop, and the team begins functioning as a cohesive group; brainstorming is used to work through issues.

- *Performing.* The team is productive and meeting its goals; members have learned to collaborate and work together.

At some point in the group process, individual members may leave the group. When that happens, the team must come together and decide how to work without the team member. This is sometimes called *adjourning*. The process of forming, storming, norming, and performing may start again.

Figure 12-2 Psychologist Bruce Tuckman described a group-development process that includes four stages.

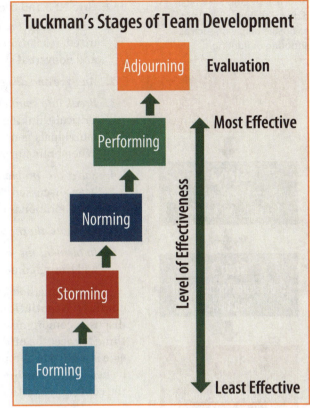

Goodheart-Willcox Publisher

Conflict Resolution

It is a fact of life that you will eventually be confronted with conflict in the workplace. **Conflict** is a strong disagreement between two or more people or a difference that prevents agreement. However, conflict is not always negative. Sometimes creative solutions can result from the interactions of people who disagree on a subject. If handled well, conflicts can strengthen the bonds between group members. Learning from disputes can help the group avoid similar conflicts in the future. However, if the conflict is not fully resolved, it can result in a recurring problem. It can throw a group off course and be destructive for the team.

When conflict arises in a group, some team members ignore it and show passive behavior. *Passive behavior* is accepting the things that happen without trying to change them. These people ignore the conflict and act as if it doesn't exist. Other members recognize the conflict and show aggressive behavior. *Aggressive behavior* is expressing individual needs with little interest or respect for the needs of others. Still other team members respond to the conflict and show assertive behavior. *Assertive behavior* is expressing personal opinions while showing respect for others.

Conflict management is the process of recognizing and resolving disputes. **Conflict-resolution skills** are the skills required to resolve a situation in which a disagreement could lead to hostile behavior, such as shouting or fighting.

Figure 12-3 Conflict-resolution skills are the skills required to resolve a situation in which a disagreement could lead to hostile behavior, such as shouting or fighting.

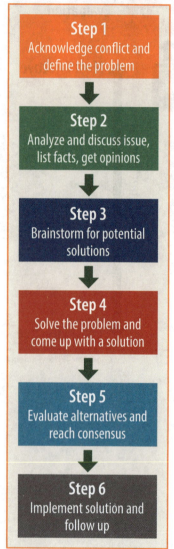

Step 1
Acknowledge conflict and define the problem

Step 2
Analyze and discuss issue, list facts, get opinions

Step 3
Brainstorm for potential solutions

Step 4
Solve the problem and come up with a solution

Step 5
Evaluate alternatives and reach consensus

Step 6
Implement solution and follow up

Goodheart-Willcox Publisher

A conflict-resolution model can be used to help develop these skills and solve the situation of disagreement. An example of a conflict-resolution model is illustrated in Figure 12-3 and is explained as follows.

1. *Acknowledge the conflict and define the problem.* If the conflict is not recognized, resolution cannot happen. Team members should apply positive verbal and nonverbal skills during this stage.

2. *Analyze and discuss the issue.* List the facts and get opinions on the issue.

3. *Break into smaller groups or brainstorm as the full group for potential solutions.* Critical-thinking skills are required. *Brainstorming* is group discussion in which individuals generate as many ideas as possible within a set amount of time. When brainstorming, there are no bad ideas; all are listed for consideration.

4. *Solve the problem and come up with solution.* After all alternatives have been discussed, it should be possible to recommend one or more solutions. Collaboration is needed from all involved.

5. *Evaluate alternatives and reach consensus.* All involved agree on a decision.

6. *Implement the solution and then follow up.* The solution or process is applied and the outcome is reviewed.

Formal methods, such as negotiation or mediation, are required to settle some conflicts. **Negotiation** is when individuals involved in a conflict come together to discuss a compromise. During negotiation, both parties are willing to give up something to meet the other party in the middle. For extreme conflicts in which neither side is willing to compromise and an agreement cannot be reached, mediation may be needed. **Mediation** is the inclusion of a neutral person, called a *mediator*, to help the conflicting parties resolve their dispute and reach an agreement.

Difficult People

A difficult person is a person who resists cooperation and forces his or her opinions on others. A *difficult employee* is a person who does not behave in a professional manner in the workplace. At some point in your career, you will encounter a difficult coworker. Difficult people are hard to please, unkind, or argumentative. They may criticize everything and everybody. They may think they are never wrong or always need to have the last word on every issue. Difficult people can be annoying or, more seriously, they can undermine another person's career.

One familiar type of difficult person is the *complainer*. The complainer never likes what the team is doing or the temperature in the room. Complainers blame others when something goes wrong or they are unable to get the job done or perform as required. These people are obnoxious and hard to please. A private discussion with a complainer may help eliminate the situation. It might be a personality issue that needs to be brought under control in the workplace.

The *angry* coworker is another example of a difficult personality. Angry coworkers may display temper outbursts when things go off course, use profanity in conversations with others, or generally show aggressive behavior. This type of negative behavior in the workplace must be addressed so it does not escalate. If you encounter an angry coworker, it is important to remain calm. If the other person is agitated, it will not help the situation if you become agitated as well. The person should be approached by stating the issue and avoiding personal comments. Using the conflict-resolution model can be helpful. If a solution cannot be found, or if you feel you are being threatened or are otherwise in danger, seek help from the human resources department.

One extreme type of difficult person is a *bully*. A bully is someone who is repeatedly unkind and cruel to another person who is perceived as weaker. The act of being a bully is called *bullying*. A bully may steal ideas, publicly criticize or humiliate others, or use abusive language. He or she may sabotage somebody's work to make them look bad. A bully may harass or even threaten someone with violence, both of which are illegal. If bullying happens to you, document the time and place of each incident of bullying and describe the behavior. Look for others who witnessed the incident, and include their names in your documentation. If the bullying behavior does not stop, take your documentation to the human resources department and seek assistance in resolving the situation.

When dealing with difficult coworkers, show professionalism. Try to stay focused on the issue and keep emotions out of the conversation. Avoid saying "you" to the other person, as it sounds accusatory. There are times when it is appropriate to just ignore a difficult person. Removing yourself from the situation can sometimes be the best solution. However, difficult people who threaten the success of the business or your personal well-being must be addressed.

Case Study

Team Conflict

Featureflash Photo Agency/Shutterstock.com

Steve Jobs, the cofounder and former chairman and CEO of Apple, Inc., once said, "…through the team, through that incredibly talented group of people bumping up against each other, having arguments, having fights sometimes, making some noise, and working together, they polish each other, they polish the ideas…" This quote came from his telling of a parable about teamwork based on something that happened to him as a child. He had befriended a widower who lived down the block from Jobs. One day, the man showed Jobs a rock tumbler. They went into the backyard and found some common, unattractive rocks and put them into the electric tumbler with some liquid and grit. They turned it on, and the tumbler began rotating. The man told Jobs to come back the next day. When Jobs came back, they opened the tumbler and removed "amazingly beautiful, polished rocks." The rocks rubbing against each other had produced a beautiful item. Jobs kept that incident in his mind as a metaphor for how conflict can help make a team produce a better outcome.

1. How do you think the parable of the rock tumbler relates to what happens in the group development process?

2. Jobs was told to return the next day to see the rocks. What lesson regarding the conflict-resolution model can be learned from Jobs having to come back to the rock tumbler a day later?

3. The rock tumbler parable implies that Jobs allowed his teams to solve their own issues. What style of leadership do you think Steve Jobs practiced?

4. How did Jobs' view of teamwork impact his professional image?

Bullies are people who are repeatedly unkind and cruel to another person who is perceived as weaker.

lightwavemedia/Shutterstock.com

Avoid becoming a difficult person. It is okay to complain and offer solutions for situations that need correcting, but becoming a difficult person is unacceptable. Disagreeing with others in a professional manner can create great outcomes and is actually needed in the workplace. However, displaying anger and creating a hostile environment is behavior that can cost you your job.

Leadership

Leadership is the ability to influence others to reach a goal. Examples of common leadership characteristics include honesty, competence, self-confidence, communication skills, problem-solving skills, and dependability. The ability to set goals, follow through on tasks, and be forward-thinking are also important leadership behaviors.

Employers seek employees who have leadership skills. Individuals who possess leadership skills are people who influence others, have ideas and solutions for challenges, and set examples for behavior. You don't have to be in a *leadership position* to exhibit *leadership skills*.

An example of a leadership position is a manager or director of a team. Being in a leadership position is not always an easy job. Some team members can be easy to work with, but others can be difficult. Leaders have to be able to work with different personalities and motivate the group to accomplish its goals. Each leader has an individual style or may develop a style based on the personalities of the team.

Three common leadership styles are democratic, autocratic, and laissez-faire, as seen in Figure 12-4. In the *democratic* leadership style, the leader shares decision-making with the group. Democratic leaders encourage other team members to participate in the leadership process. Other leaders use the autocratic style. In the *autocratic* leadership style, the leader maintains all of the power within a team. The last common type of leadership is laissez-faire. The *laissez-faire* leadership style is a hands-off approach to leadership. This style leaves the decision-making to the group.

Figure 12-4 Each leader has an individual style or may develop a style based on the personalities of the team.

Common Leadership Styles	
Leadership Style	**Characteristics**
Democratic	• Open and collegial • Invited participation from team • Shares decision-making with team members
Autocratic	• Maintains power within the group • Keeps close control over the members of the team • Makes all decisions for the group
Laissez-faire	• Hands-off approach • Little to no direction is provided • Makes decisions only if requested by the team

Goodheart-Willcox Publisher

SUMMARY

- **(LO 12-1) Describe teams in the workplace.**
  A team is a group of two or more people who work together to achieve a common goal. A team may be structured as formal or informal. Two types of teams are functional and cross-functional.

- **(LO 12-2) List the steps of the conflict-resolution model.**
  Conflict-resolution skills are the skills required to resolve a situation in which a disagreement could lead to hostile behavior, such as shouting or fighting. The steps of conflict resolution are acknowledge the conflict and define the problem; analyze and discuss the issue; break into smaller groups or brainstorm as a full group for potential solutions; solve the problem and come up with a solution; evaluate alternatives and reach consensus; and implement the solution and then follow up.

- **(LO 12-3) Identify examples of behaviors exhibited by difficult people.**
  A difficult person is a person who resists cooperation and forces his or her opinions on others. A difficult employee is a person who does not behave in a professional manner in the workplace. Difficult employees, and difficult people in general, are hard to please, unkind, or argumentative. Focusing on the issues and keeping emotions in check will help when dealing with difficult people. Ignoring the person may be the best course of action. If at any point a difficult person becomes a bully or becomes aggressive in the workplace, human resources should be contacted.

- **(LO 12-4) Describe leadership in the workplace.**
  Leadership is the ability to influence others to reach a goal. The characteristics of leadership include certain traits, such as honesty, competence, self-confidence, communication skills, problem-solving skills, and dependability. Each leader has an individual style or may develop a style based on the personalities of the team. Three common leadership styles are democratic, autocratic, and laissez-faire.

GLOSSARY TERMS

Visit the G-W Learning companion website at **www.g-wlearning.com/careereducation/** to review the following glossary terms.

collaboration skills	leadership
conflict	mediation
conflict management	negotiation
conflict-resolution skills	team
group dynamics	teamwork

REVIEW

1. Describe teams in the workplace.

2. Discuss how group dynamics affect team performance.

3. List the steps of the conflict-resolution model.

4. Identify examples of behaviors exhibited by difficult people.

5. Describe leadership in the workplace.

APPLICATION

1. List characteristics you posses that demonstrate to others that you are a team player.

2. Identify the role you typically play in your work or social group and describe how you execute that role.

3. Identify examples of teams to which you belong—these could be work-related or social teams. Next, describe the stage of formation the group has reached according to Tuckman's group-development process.

4. At some point in the group process, individual members will probably leave the group and the team must come together and decide how to work without the team member. This is sometimes called adjourning. Recall a situation in which an important player left a team of which you were a part. Describe the aftermath of the person leaving.

5. Describe a workplace conflict in which you were involved. Using the conflict-resolution model, make a list of actions that could have helped solve the conflict.

6. List one or two people you know personally or professionally whom you would classify as difficult and examples of this person's behavior that make him or her difficult.

7. Describe a time in which you encountered a bully. How did you handle the situation?

8. Most of us have at least one aspect of our personality that does not appeal to everyone. As the old adage says, "You cannot please everyone." Describe a time when coworkers would have described you as a difficult person.

9. Recall a time when you were assigned to a leadership position. In what ways were you successful and unsuccessful as a leader?

10. Three common leadership styles are democratic, autocratic, and laissez-faire. Identify a manager you have worked with and the style that person has adopted. Explain your opinion of how the style works or does not work for the team.

INTERNET ACTIVITY

Conflict Management. One of the goals of conflict management is to minimize the negative outcomes that conflicts in the workplace can cause. Conduct research on conflict management. Summarize what you learned that could help you in your career or personal life.

SKILLS PRACTICE

Visit the G-W Learning companion website at **www.g-wlearning.com/careereducation/** to access and complete the following soft skills practice activities:

Activity SS12-1 Icebreakers. Icebreakers are a good opportunity for team members to meet and get to know one another. Open the SS12-1 file, and create a list of icebreaker questions.

Activity SS12-2 Teamwork Skills. Being a team player is a soft skill that is important to career success. Open the SS12-2 file, and rate your personal teamwork skills.

CHAPTER 13

Diversity

Monkey Business Images/Shutterstock.com

BEFORE YOU READ

Visit the G-W Learning companion website to view a video about soft skills. The video is available at **www.g-wlearning.com/careereducation/**

LEARNING OUTCOMES

On completion of this chapter, prepare to:

13-1 Cite examples of factors that make up a diverse workplace.

13-2 Discuss cultural awareness, cultural intelligence, and cultural competency.

13-3 Describe how clear and successful communication across different cultures can be accomplished in the workplace.

13-4 Identify benefits of diversity for a business or organization.

Diversity in the Workplace

Diversity means having representatives from different backgrounds, cultures, or demographics in a group. It includes age, race, nationality, gender, mental ability, physical ability, and other qualities that make an individual unique.

In order to fully understand and embrace diversity, culture must be understood. **Culture** is the shared beliefs, customs, practices, and social behaviors of a particular group. Often, culture is associated with a nation or with ethnicity, but it may be associated with a region or other qualification.

A **stereotype** is a belief or generalization about a group of people with a given set of characteristics. By incorrectly assuming that all people within a certain group have the same quality or characteristic, the value and experience of each individual is ignored. Diversity benefits businesses only when the unique qualities of individuals are recognized and put to their best use.

Inclusion is the practice of recognizing, accepting, valuing, and respecting diversity. It is the act of involving all people from your work or social circles in responsibilities, functions, or activities. Inclusion means accepting diverse people who are different in gender, race, mental or physical disability, generation (age), or other qualities that make an individual unique.

Ethnicity is related to the foods, customs, clothing, beliefs, and other factors that make up a person's culture.

CHRISTIAN DE ARAUJO/Shutterstock.com

Gender

The US workforce is composed of all genders. Today, just under half of the workforce is female. Some fields or careers tend to consist mostly of males, while some fields tend to consist mostly of females. However, all genders must have equal opportunities in all fields.

Gender discrimination is any action that denies opportunities, privileges, or rewards based on a person's gender. It may be committed against a single person or a group of people. All people are protected against gender discrimination by law.

According to the federal government, *gender identity* is a person's internal sense of being male or female. The way in which this is expressed is frequently called *gender expression*. One's gender expression may or may not conform to the social roles associated with a particular sex. For example, a person who identifies as *transgender* has a gender identity that is different from his or her sex at birth.

Race

Race and ethnicity are often confused, and there is disagreement on the definitions of each. Generally, **ethnicity** is the culture with which a person identifies, such as South Asian, Mexican, English, or German. Ethnicity is related to the foods, customs, clothing, beliefs, and other factors that make up a person's culture. *Race*, on the other hand, is generally defined as a large group of people who share history, ancestry, and physical traits.

A person may have more than one ethnicity. For example, the race of a child born to Asian parents in China is Asian. Suppose, however, that child is adopted by an African-American family in America. The child will grow up in both American and African-American cultures and likely will identify with those ethnicities, but the child's race remains Asian. As the child matures, he or she may become interested in Chinese culture. This may lead the child to identify with American, African-American, and Chinese ethnicities.

The federal government uses the designations shown in Figure 13-1 to categorize US citizens, resident aliens, and other eligible noncitizens by race. These designations are based on a social definition of race as generally recognized in the United States. Since 2010, the US Census has allowed the selection of multiple racial categories. People who identify with more than one race are referred to as *multiracial* individuals. Multiracial individuals are a growing segment of the population. Data gathered through the 2010 census showed that the population of multiracial individuals grew at a higher percentage than the population of single-race individuals.

Certain employment laws mandate diversity. For example, the US government passed the *Civil Rights Act of 1964*, which ended segregation in workplaces and public schools, as well as unequal voting requirements. This made it illegal to discriminate against a person based on his or her race, color, religion, gender, or national origin.

Disability

According to the *Americans with Disabilities Act (ADA)*, a **disability** is a physical or mental impairment that substantially limits one or more of a person's major life activities. The ADA is a federal civil rights law that was enacted in 1990. It prohibits discrimination against any person with a disability in all areas of public life, including in the workplace.

The same employment opportunities and benefits available to those without disabilities must be available to those with disabilities. Prior to the ADA, there were no requirements to make buildings accessible to those with disabilities. For example, a ramp or lift is now required to allow a person with a mobility disability to bypass stairs.

Reasonable measures must be taken to enable an employee with a disability to participate and function in the essential work activities of his or her position. However, reasonable measures go beyond ramps and elevators. Technological accessibility is equally important. Tools such as screen readers, alternative text descriptions (alt text), text-to-speech applications, and Braille versions of information make it possible for those with disabilities to achieve the same level of efficiency as those without disabilities. Provisions of the act also require businesses to take reasonable measures to communicate with those who have vision, hearing, or speech impairments.

Figure 13-1 The federal government uses these designations to categorize US citizens, resident aliens, and other eligible noncitizens by race.

Designations of Race as Defined by the Federal Government	
Race Designation	**Description**
Hispanic or Latino	A person of Cuban, Mexican, Puerto Rican, South or Central American, or other Spanish culture or origin, regardless of race.
American Indian or Alaska Native	A person having origins in any of the original peoples of North and South America (including Central America) who maintains cultural identification through tribal affiliation or community attachment.
Asian	A person having origins in any of the original peoples of the Far East, Southeast Asia, or the Indian Subcontinent, including, for example, Cambodia, China, India, Japan, Korea, Malaysia, Pakistan, the Philippine Islands, Thailand, and Vietnam.
Black or African-American	A person having origins in any of the black racial groups of Africa.
Native Hawaiian or Other Pacific Islander	A person having origins in any of the original peoples of Hawaii, Guam, Samoa, or other Pacific Islands.
White	A person having origins in any of the original peoples of Europe, the Middle East, or North Africa.

Source: US Census Bureau; Goodheart-Willcox Publisher

Age

In 1967, the United States passed the *Age Discrimination in Employment Act*, which made it illegal to discriminate against a person 40 or more years of age. This law prohibits discrimination in promotions, wages, hiring, benefits, layoffs, and termination. It also eliminated mandatory retirement in most occupations. A person's age does not dictate his or her abilities. Even though an employee may be older, it does not mean that he or she cannot do the same work as a younger worker.

An *age-neutral* environment embraces workers of all ages and takes advantage of the values and strengths each generation brings to the workplace. It embraces the differences that each generation brings to the situation. The benefits of an age-neutral workforce include flexibility, creativity, a broad customer base, and diverse perspectives. Each generation's talents and skills should be blended to work toward the common goal.

In today's workforce, people of many ages and generations work together. A **generation** is a group of people who were born and lived during the same time period. A **multigenerational workforce** consists of employees who represent multiple age groups and generations. It is not uncommon to see people from age 16 to 70 working at similar jobs in a place of employment.

Currently, there are at least five recognized generations, as shown in Figure 13-2. People within certain age groups have witnessed the same historic events, seen the evolution of certain technologies, and have other shared life experiences. A person's age when witnessing certain events can affect the impact those events have on a person's life. For example, a presidential election will leave a different impression on a 10-year-old person than it will on a 30-year-old person. Such events help shape a person's values and beliefs, which translates into the way he or she behaves and works with others.

Some critics say that categorizing people by the year they are born is stereotyping. Labeling an individual as a member of a generation places that person in an arbitrary group strictly based on birth year without considering personal characteristics, cultures, or other factors. It ignores ethnicity and personal traits that make people who they are. The practice of classification by generation can be considered offensive by some individuals.

Generalizations about age and generations should not be used to stereotype people in a negative manner, such as job discrimination. However, using it in a non-offensive manner can be considered acceptable, such as marketers who use age and generations as *positive stereotypes* to help determine customer needs for products and services.

Group dynamics are the interacting forces within a group or team, including the attitudes, behaviors, and personalities of all members. The multigenerational workforce has influenced group dynamics and presented certain challenges for employees and employers. Some of those challenges are stereotyping, communication differences, and cultural expectations.

Figure 13-2 A generation is a group of people who were born and lived during the same time period.

Commonly Used Categories of Generations in the United States	
Generational Title	**Year of Birth**
iGeneration (Generation Z)	1996–present
Millennial Generation (Generation Y)	1980–1995
Generation X	1965–1980
Baby Boom Generation	1946–1964
Silent Generation	1928–1945

Goodheart-Willcox Publisher

Stereotypes

Diversity should never be a barrier to cooperation or communication, nor should it create situations of stereotyping. Often, a stereotype is untrue and has a negative meaning. For example, older workers may think that younger workers are "job-hoppers" if they change jobs frequently. The reality may be they are looking for a better opportunity and work-life balance. A **work-life balance** is the amount of time spent at work compared to the amount of time spent with family and friends and engaged in leisure activities.

Alternatively, younger workers may think that older workers do not like change because they stay in one job for years and never change employers. Younger workers may think it is "boring" not to change employment. However, older workers may like their jobs. They worked to earn their positions, and they may be happy with their status in the company. Their reason for staying is not related to disliking or fearing change. In both instances, the stereotype is incorrect.

Generational stereotypes can lead to misunderstandings and negatively influence the dynamics of a team. This can create a multitude of issues including bias. *Bias* is a tendency to believe that some ideas or people are better than others, which often results in acting unfairly and creates negative self-worth for team members. Negative stereotyping is never acceptable and should be actively discouraged in the work environment.

Communication

Communication issues between generations in the workplace can be eliminated through the exchanging of ideas. Each team member should be open with coworkers about the type of communication that is better for him or her. Honest discussion can eliminate future misunderstandings. Listening to each other is an important part of the communication process.

For example, younger workers may prefer to e-mail coworkers as their primary means of communication. Alternatively, older workers may prefer face-to-face communication when interacting with a coworker. These are basic workplace interactions that can present challenges, lead to misunderstandings, and may project a perceived lack of respect when none is intended. Establishing expectations is a simple way to demonstrate respect and cooperation.

Cultural Expectations

Culture is the shared beliefs, customs, practices, and social behaviors of a particular group. Each generation has expectations about *workplace culture* based on their past work experiences. Employers influence the culture of their businesses and the people who work for them.

Historically, it was a common cultural workplace expectation to judge a person's performance by how many hours he or she put in at the office. The output of a person's work was not necessarily the primary measure. If the person was in the office nine or ten hours each day and came in on the weekends, he or she may have been seen as a hard worker and valuable to the company. This is the environment in which many older workers "grew up" within their industries. As a result, that is the *culture* they expect.

On the other hand, younger workers may not necessarily equate hours in the office to productivity. Younger workers are more likely to embrace mobile technologies that allow them to work anywhere, not just in the office.

In both instances, the culture of the generation is different. Through discussion of expectations for company culture, issues can be resolved before they erupt.

Culture

Culture influences how people respond to the communication and behavior of individuals and organizations. It affects how people think, work, and interact with others.

Embracing diversity requires the development of one's cultural awareness, cultural intelligence, and cultural competency.

Cultural Awareness

Cultural awareness is an understanding of the differences and similarities between one's personal culture and the culture of another person or group. In order to have cultural awareness, you must first understand your own culture. How do you dress, and do others around you dress similarly? Food is often an important part of culture. Do you and your family eat the same foods as most people who live in your community? It is important to learn how your personal culture influences how you live each day and the life decisions you make. Once you understand your own culture, you can begin to develop cultural awareness toward others.

Case Study

K2 images/Shutterstock.com

Diversity

Sonia Sotomayor grew up in the housing projects of the South Bronx. From a very early age, she knew that she wanted a career in law. A self-proclaimed example of affirmative action, Sotomayor attended the prestigious Princeton and Yale Universities in pursuit of her chosen career. While in college and law school, she was an active voice for the issues and concerns of minority students.

After graduating, she worked as an assistant district attorney in New York and eventually went into private practice. She was honored with nominations to both the US District Court and US Court of Appeals for the Second Circuit. While sitting on the Second Circuit, she was a member of the Task Force on Gender, Racial and Ethnic Fairness in the Courts.

In 2009, Sonia Sotomayor became the first Hispanic woman appointed to the Supreme Court. From this influential position, she continues to advocate for equality and diversity, which includes diversity of justices sitting on the Supreme Court. Many of her public speeches and addresses highlight the importance and benefits of diversity. "I want to state upfront, unequivocally and without doubt: I do not believe that any racial, ethnic or gender group has an advantage in sound judging. I do believe that every person has an equal opportunity to be a good and wise judge, regardless of their background or life experiences."

1. What types of stereotyping do you think Sotomayor experienced as a Hispanic appointed to the Supreme Court?

2. What types of stereotyping do you think Sotomayor experienced as the first Hispanic *woman* appointed to the Supreme Court?

3. Cite an example of a benefit that Sotomayor's diversity brought to the Supreme Court.

4. How has being an advocate for diversity impacted Justice Sotomayor's professional image?

Etiquette dictates that individuals be sensitive to the cultures of others. This is often referred to as *cultural sensitivity*. A failure to be sensitive to the cultures of others can lead to miscommunication, errors, missed opportunities, hurt feelings, and even lost business.

For example, in the United States, it is common to give someone you meet in business your business card. This exchange is simple without any significance attached to how it is done. It is also not uncommon to make notes on the card, such as an area or product of interest or a best time to make contact. To be sure not to lose it, the person receiving the card may immediately tuck it into a wallet and then slip the wallet into a pocket. There is very little chance for anything to go wrong with this exchange, as long as both people are vested in American culture.

However, in Asia the exchange of a business card is very important. In these cultures, the business card is an extension of the person (especially his or her face), and the process of exchanging cards is considered a ceremony. The card should be offered by holding it in front of you with both hands as you bow slightly, and it should be accepted in the same way.

Even where the card is grasped is important, as the company name or logo or the person's name should never be covered. The person accepting the card should spend a few seconds inspecting the card, holding it over a dedicated business card holder. This is a sign of respect. The card should remain visible for the duration of the meeting, and then carefully placed in the holder. The card should never be placed in your back pocket as this is a sign of disrespect. You would be sitting on the card and, by extension, sitting on the person. It is also extremely disrespectful to write on the card or otherwise damage it.

Continual cultural awareness to interact and exchange ideas with individuals from diverse cultural settings is necessary in the workplace. As can be seen in the examples of exchanging business cards, in one culture this is a simple process, but in another culture it is a very formal process. If the formal process is not followed, the results could lead to misunderstandings or, worse, a failed meeting. However, cultural awareness is only part of the equation. Cultural awareness and cultural intelligence are interrelated. Through development of cultural awareness, one can acquire cultural intelligence.

Cultural Intelligence

The concept of cultural intelligence was introduced in the early 21st century. **Cultural intelligence**, often abbreviated as *CQ*, is the ability to adapt to unfamiliar cultural situations. It is *not* a measure of the intellectual capability of a person or the intelligence of those in a particular culture. An individual with a high cultural intelligence is aware of values, beliefs, and attitudes of those from a different culture and can change personal behaviors to better match. Since the ability to change personal behaviors requires cultural awareness, the link between cultural awareness and cultural intelligence is inherent.

Cultural intelligence is important to the overall success and survival of a community. By developing a high CQ, a person is better able to communicate and interact with others. For example, in some Middle Eastern cultures, it is acceptable to negotiate the price of a product. This is called *haggling*. While haggling is not common in American culture as a whole, there may be some communities or neighborhoods that have a culture where haggling is accepted. It may be considered rude not to follow the cultural norm where applicable. Having a high cultural intelligence for those communities helps support the economic well-being of businesses located there and shows respect for their values and customers.

A high cultural intelligence also helps to identify barriers in cross-cultural relationships. For example, many businesses in Western culture respect the *go-getter*, someone who can take charge of a meeting and close the deal or get the job done in short order. This person typically has a *Type A* personality. He or she is very outgoing, has a great amount of drive or ambition to succeed, has a need for control, and quickly moves from a completed task to the next task.

In China, however, this type of behavior has no value. In Chinese culture, respect is given to those who can make personal connections and are interested in long-term partnerships. If a person comes into a meeting and says, "Here is what you need to do," he or she will likely offend any Chinese partners. Instead of making a demanding statement, it may be better to direct the conversation by posing a question, such as "Would you be willing to consider...?"

Cultural Competency

Cultural competency is the acknowledgment of cultural differences and the ability to adapt one's communication style to successfully send and receive messages despite those differences. Think of cultural competency as a two-step process. The first step requires a person to be aware of cultural barriers, which is the development of cultural awareness. The second step requires taking necessary precautions to overcome those barriers, which is applying cultural intelligence.

For example, corporations operating on a global scale often hold meetings with representatives from different countries. The acknowledgment of a potential language or cultural barrier is the successful completion of the first step. If a language barrier does exist, the culturally competent action is to have an interpreter present to avoid any miscommunication, which completes the second step of the process. An *interpreter* is a person who translates conversations between individuals who do not speak the same language.

Achieving cultural competence may not always be an easy task. In general, treating people with respect and patience and using best practices in the workplace will ultimately help in attaining cultural competence.

Intercultural Communication

Intercultural communication is the process of sending and receiving messages between people of various cultures. The communication process is a series of actions on the part of the sender and the receiver of a message, as well as the path of the message.

The sender creates and sends the message. The receiver is the person who reads, hears, or sees the message. Once the message is received, it is translated into terms the receiver can understand. When the sender and receiver are from different cultures, the message may not be translated as intended. Each party translates the message based on his or her own culture and beliefs, which may differ from each other. For example, in the United States a topic is considered "tabled" if it is put off for another time. In contrast, the same phrase in Great Britain means to "bring it to the table" for discussion. If this phrase is part of a message between two people from different cultures, a misunderstanding could occur.

Language is often a barrier to intercultural communication. **English as a Second Language (ESL)** is the field of education concerned with teaching English to those whose native language is not English. This field may also be known as *English as a Foreign Language (EFL)*, especially outside of the United States.

People who do not speak English, or do not speak it fluently, may take ESL classes to learn how to more effectively communicate using the English language. Likewise, a native English speaker living or working in a foreign country may learn to speak the language of the country in order to communicate as clearly as possible and avoid misunderstandings.

Working in a diverse environment requires that individuals learn how to communicate clearly and concisely. This sometimes means taking extra time and patience to establish and maintain working relationships. Clear and successful communication can be accomplished through careful listening, clear speech, and awareness of nonverbal communication.

Careful Listening

It is courteous to listen to each person with whom you come in contact. *Listening* is the process of hearing speech and evaluating the message. It is one of the most important skills you will use in your career. When listening to diverse individuals, extra attention needs to be given. English may not be a person's native language. Imagine yourself in another country trying to speak a foreign language. It could be frustrating trying to express a thought or idea if you are not versed in the language. Show empathy to others who are in that situation with you.

Just as when listening to a friend or family member, these basic courtesies should be applied when listening to coworkers from different cultures:

- Do not interrupt.
- Ask for clarification for any point you do not understand.
- Watch for nonverbal cues.
- Concentrate on what the person is saying.
- Provide appropriate feedback.

Clear Speech

When communicating with others whose native language is not English, it is important to speak clearly. Using simple language and short sentences can help avoid misunderstandings. It is helpful to speak slowly, and clearly pronounce words. Be polite and use common courtesies. If the person does not seem to understand what you have said, try to rephrase. Speaking loudly will not make the person understand what you are saying.

Nonverbal Communication

As discussed in Chapter 7, body language, eye contact, touch, and personal space play an important role in communication. All cultures assign specific meanings to nonverbal behavior, and often, two cultures do not always give the same meaning to an action. Being aware of nonverbal communication can help eliminate barriers when dealing with people from other cultures.

For example, direct eye contact is not acceptable in some cultures while it is favorable in others. Similarly, different cultures have varying standards of how much personal space should be given to other people. In some cases, shaking hands may be inappropriate when meeting someone from one culture, while it is common in others.

If you will be interacting with someone from another culture, conduct research to understand what body language cues will be expected by that person. Social etiquette in the other culture may be very different from what you are used to. Try to understand these differences before the interaction begins.

Benefits of Diversity

A diverse workforce has many advantages. Often, diversity leads to new ideas, higher productivity, improved customer service, and a better reputation for the company.

The same employment opportunities and benefits available to those without disabilities must be available to those with disabilities.

Firma V/Shutterstock.com

New Ideas

Diversity can help organizations be more creative, be receptive to customer needs, and find new ways of completing tasks. Having a diverse workforce can help a company create products and services that may be new in the marketplace. These new ideas can generate increased revenue and employee pride. New ways of thinking and looking at business are benefits of hiring people with varied backgrounds and experiences.

Higher Productivity

In many cases, working in a diverse environment improves employee morale. This, in turn, leads to a greater desire by employees to do well for the company. Productivity and efficiency both can increase as a result.

Improved Customer Service

Customer service is an important function for businesses. All companies service a variety of customers, regardless of their language or culture. Providing excellent customer service can be a challenge when speaking with a customer who may not speak English or speak it well.

Customer service teams that provide assistance in various languages can increase sales as well as customer satisfaction. For example, by hiring employees who speak Spanish fluently, a business can better serve customers whose native language is Spanish and have limited English proficiency.

In addition, employees who receive diversity training are more capable of servicing customers from diverse backgrounds. They are generally more sensitive to people from other cultures and are more culturally competent, so they better understand how to interpret specific needs.

Reputation

Increasing diversity in the workforce naturally increases the pool of potential qualified candidates. This can result in a more effective workforce. Also, having a diverse workforce helps to improve the reputation of the company. The company can become known to customers and potential employees as one that embraces diversity. This reputation can serve to draw potential employees to the company. It can also draw customers to the company who value diversity, as well as those who have needs they hope can be serviced by a company with a diverse workforce.

SUMMARY

- **(LO 13-1) Cite examples of factors that make up a diverse workplace.**
  Diversity means having representatives from different backgrounds, cultures, or demographics. It includes age, race, nationality, gender, mental ability, physical ability, and other qualities that make an individual unique.

- **(LO 13-2) Discuss cultural awareness, cultural intelligence, and cultural competency.**
  Cultural awareness is an understanding of the differences and similarities between one's personal culture and the culture of another person or group. In order to have cultural awareness, you must first understand your own culture. Cultural intelligence is the ability to adapt to unfamiliar cultural situations. It is *not* a measure of the intellectual capability of a person or the intelligence of those in a particular culture. Cultural competency is the acknowledgment of cultural differences and the ability to adapt one's communication style to successfully send and receive messages despite those differences.

- **(LO 13-3) Describe how clear and successful communication across different cultures can be accomplished in the workplace.**
  Working in a diverse environment requires that individuals learn how to communicate clearly and concisely. Clear and successful communication can be accomplished through careful listening, clear speech, and awareness of nonverbal communication.

- **(LO 13-4) Identify benefits of diversity for a business or organization.**
  A diverse workforce has many advantages. Often, diversity leads to increased creativity, productivity, and customer service, as well as a favorable reputation in the industry.

GLOSSARY TERMS

Visit the G-W Learning companion website at **www.g-wlearning.com/careereducation/** to review the following glossary terms.

cultural awareness	ethnicity
cultural competency	generation
cultural intelligence	inclusion
culture	intercultural communication
disability	multigenerational workforce
diversity	stereotype
English as a Second Language (ESL)	work-life balance

REVIEW

1. Cite factors that make up a diverse workplace.

2. Discuss cultural awareness, cultural intelligence, and cultural competency.

3. Explain why cultural intelligence is important to the overall success and survival of a community.

4. Describe how clear and successful communication can be accomplished in the workplace.

5. How does diversity benefit a workplace?

APPLICATION

1. Recall a workplace or school situation in which you witnessed stereotyping or bias toward another individual. Describe what you think was the outcome for that person's self-worth as well as the dynamics of the individual's peers.

2. Observe the accommodations that have been made for people with disabilities in your work or school. Compile your findings in a list. Identify any additional accommodations that you think should be made.

3. Discuss your thoughts about reporting to a supervisor who is younger than you. How would it be different from reporting to someone your age or older?

4. Describe your experience with a multigenerational team or collaboration. What were some of the positive elements that you took away from the interaction?

5. Marketers often use age and generations as positive stereotypes to help determine customer needs. List examples of positive stereotypes with which you are familiar.

6. Identify your generation and discuss personal characteristics you think are common to those in your age group. Compare some of those characteristics with your parents' generation.

7. Explain your ideal work-life balance.

8. Cultural competence is a combination of a person's cultural awareness and cultural intelligence. Based on this description, how culturally competent are you?

9. Describe the culture in which you were raised and how it has played a role in your personality.

10. Think of your last group project. Identify the unique qualities (gender, race, mental or physical disability, age, ethnicity) of the group members. Explain how the diversity of the group impacted the collaboration, general interactions, and project completion.

INTERNET ACTIVITY

Cultural intelligence (CQ). Cultural intelligence (CQ) is the ability to adapt to unfamiliar cultural situations. Conduct an Internet search for a Cultural Intelligence (CQ) quiz. Take the test and evaluate your score.

SKILLS PRACTICE

Visit the G-W Learning companion website at **www.g-wlearning.com/careereducation/** to access and complete the following soft skills practice activities:

Activity SS13-1 Cultural Awareness. In order to have cultural awareness, an individual must first understand his or her own culture. Open the SS13-1 file, and complete the activity so that you may reflect on your personal culture.

Activity SS13-2 Cultural Intelligence. Cultural intelligence, often abbreviated as CQ, is the ability to adapt to unfamiliar cultural situations. Open the SS13-2 file, and rate your behaviors that contribute to your CQ.

CHAPTER 14

Confidence

Olga Danylenko/Shutterstock.com

AFTER YOU READ

After you have finished reading this chapter, see what you have learned about soft skills by taking a posttest. The soft skills posttest is available at **www.g-wlearning.com/careereducation/**

LEARNING OUTCOMES

On completion of this chapter, prepare to:

14-1 Discuss the relationship between self-confidence and self-esteem.

14-2 Identify examples of actions necessary for professional advancement.

14-3 Describe the importance of having realistic career expectations.

Self-esteem is your sense of self-worth and how you see yourself when you look in the mirror.

Bajrich/Shutterstock.com

Self-Confidence

An important element of an individual's professional image is self-confidence. **Self-confidence** is being certain and secure about one's own abilities and judgment. People with self-confidence believe in their ability to perform or make something positive happen in a situation. These individuals know what they are good at doing and how to best use their abilities to achieve goals. Self-confident individuals exhibit confidence in their positions and are aware of their value to the organization for which they work. Employers seek employees who demonstrate confidence in their actions and communication. Managers depend on their staff to perform job activities, use judgment, and deliver what is promised without constant supervision.

A person's self-confidence is affected by his or her self-talk. *Self-talk* is the practice of talking to oneself, either silently or aloud. This can often influence how a person feels about himself or herself. Positive self-talk includes reinforcement of one's appearance, skills, or other qualities. Negative self-talk consists of disparaging comments. It is common to participate in negative self-talk when things do not go the way you intended. Negative self-talk can turn positive simply by choosing to believe in yourself. The more confidently you believe in yourself, the more others will believe in you.

Closely related to self-confidence is self-esteem. **Self-esteem** is how an individual feels about his or her value as a person. It is your sense of self-worth and how you see yourself when you look in the mirror. The more comfortable you are with yourself as a person, the more self-confidence you will exhibit.

Your self-esteem is also influenced by your self-image. **Self-image** is the way a person thinks about himself or herself, including personal abilities, appearance, and other people's perceptions. Figure 14-1 lists examples of behaviors exhibited by an individual with high self-esteem versus an individual with low self-esteem.

Self-confidence and self-esteem should not be confused with arrogance. **Arrogance** is an attitude in which an individual believes he or she is better than other people. It can arise from too much or too little self-confidence or self-esteem. Arrogant people may not work well with others because they think they are more important and their ideas are better. They may exhibit a sense of superiority over coworkers and can sometimes transform into a workplace bully. Figure 14-2 lists some common behaviors of arrogant people.

Figure 14-1 Self-esteem is how an individual feels about his or her value as a person.

Self-Esteem Behaviors	
High Self-Esteem	**Low Self-Esteem**
Firmly believes in set values and principles	Engages in severe self-criticism
Believes in own abilities to solve problems, asks for help when needed, and adapts when things do not work out as planned	Is very sensitive to external criticism
Can trust personal judgment in making decisions	Finds making decisions difficult due to a fear of making mistakes
Is not easily manipulated by others	Is overly concerned with pleasing others out of fear of disappointing them
Can empathize	Easily becomes angry or hostile even over insignificant issues
Feels equal to others	Feels insignificant
Has a sense of self-worth	Has an overall negative view on life

Goodheart-Willcox Publisher

Figure 14-2 Arrogance is an attitude in which an individual believes he or she is better than other people.

An arrogant individual is often:

- self-centered, but can be charming.
- critical of others, but rejects feedback about self.
- a self-perceived expert on everything, and disparages the knowledge and input of others.
- ingratiating with employer or manager, and belittling toward coworkers.
- the center of attention, and becomes aggravated or jealous if someone else gets attention.
- staunch in personal beliefs and perspectives, but intolerant of others whose beliefs differ.
- pleasant and kind to your face, but negative about you to others behind your back.

Goodheart-Willcox Publisher

The opposite of arrogance is humility. **Humility** means to be modest and not to think one is better than other people. People who have humility are humble in their behavior, but it does not mean they lack self-confidence. Possessing humility does not mean to be meek or have diminished self-esteem or self-image. Instead, it means treating people respectfully, being confident in your abilities, and behaving as a professional. When soft skills are mastered, some aspects of humility naturally happen. For example, simply saying "thank you" to someone demonstrates humility.

Professional Success

Many people identify self with career. A personal sense of accomplishment, satisfaction, and value can be gained from working in a chosen profession. As such, many people seek professional advancement as an indicator of success. Advancement can be measured by a promotion, new job title, or other forms of recognition that can help an individual attain desired career status. Each individual has his or her own measure of job success.

To attain advancement, it is important to exhibit confidence in personal performance and the ability to interact in the workplace. It also requires taking control of your career and learning how to effectively negotiate, manage up, self-promote, and appropriately deal with office politics within the organization.

Negotiation

"Everything is negotiable," as the saying goes, especially in the workplace. To **negotiate** is to have a formal discussion between two or more people in an attempt to reach an agreement. It is common to negotiate salary with an employer, ideas and solutions with coworkers, and work schedules with a manager.

Good negotiating requires being prepared and possessing confidence. A negotiator should be ready to discuss the details of the request, why it is reasonable, and the expected outcome for all parties. Keep in mind that each participant will have his or her own goals for the negotiation, so thorough preparation is necessary. Emotions should be kept under control and active listening should be demonstrated by each party before reacting to the opinions expressed. Self-confidence is important, but arrogance should not be involved.

Ultimatums are generally not a good solution when negotiating. However, in a competitive workplace, they may be necessary. Some situations require that the negotiator risk all and give an ultimatum, but only if he or she is willing to lose. For example, a person negotiating a salary may state that if a specific amount of money is not part of the package, he or she will decline the job offer. Sometimes this can work, but he or she must be willing to accept rejection and loss of an opportunity.

Manage Up

Manage up is a common term in the workplace. *Managing up* is the efforts of an employee to establish a working relationship with a supervisor so that his or her professional needs are met as well as the employee's own needs. It is the act of demonstrating professional behavior and working toward the goals of a supervisor and the company.

To manage up is to show basic respect for management. It is the act of maintaining a good attitude, volunteering your services when needed, and learning how to make your boss look good. Successful employees determine what the manager wants and how to show support. It includes being proactive in situations that demand attention. Knowing how to help your manager can make you an asset to the team and to the company. It can also position you for promotions when they arise.

Case Study

Library of Congress, Prints & Photographs Division, photograph by Carol M. Highsmith

Humility

Paul William "Bear" Bryant was one of the most prolific college football coaches of all time. Bryant finished his coaching career with an overall head coaching record of 323 wins. He encouraged his players to work hard, train hard, study hard, and play hard. Most of all, he encouraged them to win. Winning was important to Bear Bryant, but perhaps the most important thing was winning with humility. Bryant once said, "It's awfully important to win with humility. It's also important to lose. I hate to lose worse than anyone, but if you never lose you won't know how to act. If you lose with humility, then you can come back." By emphasizing the importance of humility to his players, Bryant helped them develop into not only champions, but well-rounded, productive workers, as well. Bryant passed away in 1983, but his legacy lives on. Scores of his players went on to great success in football, and the University of Alabama football stadium bears his name.

1. What does it mean to win with humility?

2. Why do you think Bear Bryant said it is "important to lose"?

3. How would you describe Bryant's professionalism?

4. Why do you think Bryant's professional image continues to be associated with winning?

Some people confuse "managing up" with "playing up." *Playing up* is going through the motions of building a relationship with a supervisor and displaying professional behavior, but the motivation behind the actions is not genuine. Someone who plays up to his or her superiors is only looking to gain influence and does not have the best interests of the company in mind. This is often demonstrated through flattery, insincere praise, and eager attentiveness toward a supervisor or manager. Playing up is often called *brown-nosing*.

An elevator speech is several sentences that tell who a person is, what he or she does that is of value, and why that work is important.

bikeriderlondon/Shutterstock.com

Self-Promotion

Self-promotion is the act of making coworkers, peers, managers, or potential employers aware of oneself so that personal value can be established. Many people in the workplace compete for positions within an organization. If management does not know who you are or your value to the company, you could be overlooked when promotions or other opportunities arise. Many employees who are respected as positive contributors are sometimes overlooked for promotions simply because they did not have the self-confidence to let their ambitions be known.

Self-promotion requires self-awareness. **Self-awareness** is a sense of being aware of one's feelings, behaviors, needs, and other elements that make up the whole person. In order to promote yourself to others, you have to be aware of who you are and what your ultimate goal may be in the organization.

Marketing and selling yourself, but not bragging or being arrogant, are strategies needed for self-promotion. An important part of the process is showing how you can be of value to the organization. Self-promotion can start by participating on task forces or in other activities that spotlight your contributions and accomplishments. Getting to know your manager and making sure he or she knows your value to the team is a great way to self-promote. Helping coworkers and demonstrating how you are a team player are ways to win support from peers.

For more formal self-promotion, personal branding strategies are helpful. Many professionals create their own personal branding strategy that includes an elevator speech. An **elevator speech** is several sentences that tell who a person is, what he or she does that is of value, and why that work is important. It is a brief commercial about yourself that could be told while riding in an elevator with someone from whom you want attention. This could be your manager's boss or someone from another company with whom you would like to work. The audience for an elevator speech is anyone who could help you meet your personal goals.

Office Politics

Office politics is inevitable in most organizations. *Office politics* is the behavior that individuals practice to gain advantages over others in the workplace. It is a struggle for power. Engaging in office politics, unlike self-promotion, is considered inappropriate at best and is often unethical. Some individuals believe that the more they know about company business, the more power they will have. Others want to secure a friendship with the boss or others who can help them climb the ladder for promotions. Gossipers may say unkind things about coworkers to try to make them look worse. Some workers withhold information from a coworker to maintain an advantage over him or her. Many times office politics results in a coworker being the victim of someone's negative behavior. Unfortunately, while you can avoid participating in office politics, you cannot prevent others from engaging in such behavior.

Realistic Expectations

We all have expectations for our personal and professional lives and accomplishments. If you have acquired the knowledge needed for your profession, polished your soft skills, and work hard, you should be able to be successful in your professional life. Each individual in the workplace must work to prove personal skills and worth.

Professional expectations must be realistic. It is easy to be over-confident and expect instant success, power, and respect. This is simply unrealistic. No one is *entitled* to career success; it must be earned. For example, it is not realistic to graduate from college and:

- earn a six-figure income;
- be given a senior manager position;
- expect a promotion after the first year on a job;
- get six weeks of vacation in the first year of employment;
- be given a prestigious office; or
- have a personal administrative assistant.

Striving to reach unrealistic personal and professional expectations can create psychological problems, such as stress or anxiety. These can also cause physical problems, such as not getting enough sleep or feeling ill.

Over-confidence and unrealistic expectations should not deter your success. You should have a realistic view of your abilities and worth, but also understand that there is always room for improvement. Continue to learn and expand your skills in order to increase your value as an employee, as well as the opportunities available in your career.

Position

A career plan should start with a realistic entry-level position and detail the experience and development needed to achieve each successive level. In any career, there is a starting point and usually a hierarchy that allows for upward mobility. This hierarchy is referred to as a career ladder. A *career ladder* is a sequence of work in a career field, from entry to advanced levels. Career levels are typically categorized by skill or education level, as shown in Figure 14-3.

When entering the workforce, expect your first job to be at one of the lowest-level positions. You may not start at the lowest rung on the career ladder, but it is unrealistic to start at the top or even in the middle. In order to move up the hierarchy, you will need to gain experience. Additionally, you will need to apply the skills you learned in school and demonstrate your ability to assume more responsibility and higher-level tasks.

When first entering the workforce, it is unrealistic to expect to be in a position where a direct report is available to you. *Direct reports* are coworkers who report to you. For example, as a manager, you may have an administrative assistant. However, in your first position, you will likely need to do all of the work yourself, even if this means working beyond your scheduled hours.

Salary

According to the United States Census Bureau, the median household income in the United States in 2015 was around $53,000 annually. In some professions, you will make more than this, but in some you will make less. Keep in mind, the reported average income is just that—an *average*. There will be some individuals who make quite a bit more than that figure and some who make quite a bit less.

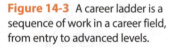

Figure 14-3 A career ladder is a sequence of work in a career field, from entry to advanced levels.

Goodheart-Willcox Publisher

The salaries of all individuals in the field are used to calculate the average salary. When starting your career, it is unrealistic to earn the average salary. In all likelihood, you will make quite a bit below the average. Depending on many factors, such as location and cost of living, you may eventually earn the reported average, but you may not.

Benefits

Benefits are noncash compensation offered to an employee in addition to a wage. Examples of benefits are paid vacation time or paid health insurance premiums. The benefits offered by a company should be evaluated as part of the process in deciding to accept or decline a job offer. However, it is important to have realistic expectations in regard to benefits. For example, if the job is working in an office all day, it is unreasonable to expect that a company car be given to you. On the other hand, if the job is a sales position that requires a great deal of travel, it may be reasonable to be offered a company car. At an entry-level sales position, however, it is likely you will be reimbursed for the mileage you drive in your own car instead.

Most companies offer some sort of paid time off (PTO), which is often generically called vacation. It is very common for a company to have a sliding scale for the number of days an employee will receive. For example, in the first year, an employee may receive one week of PTO. After that, maybe the employee may be allowed two weeks of PTO. In some companies, long-term employees are rewarded with additional PTO after a certain number of years, such as five or ten years of service. Expecting to receive three or four weeks of PTO in your first year in a company is unrealistic.

Sometimes, especially if you come to the company with several years of experience, you may be able to negotiate your benefits. You may be able to ask for additional PTO to match what you currently receive. You may also be able to negotiate other benefits and even salary. Be aware that a company is not going to offer additional benefits unless you can demonstrate a unique skill or knowledge that the company is willing to accept to offset the additional expense.

Promotion

Promotion is advancing to the next level in the company's hierarchy. Promotions must be earned; they are not automatically given. Ways to earn a promotion include showing the ability to follow company policies, demonstrating the skills needed for the higher position, and exemplifying the soft skills required to work with coworkers and subordinates.

In many cases, it is relatively easy to move from one lower rung on the hierarchy to the next rung. However, as you progress up the ladder, promotions are generally harder to achieve. Think of an inverted funnel. There are typically fewer positions the higher up the hierarchy you go, but the same number of people vying for those limited positions.

Just because promotions may be easier to achieve at the lower levels of the hierarchy, it is unrealistic to expect a promotion after only a few months. It will take time to prove your skills and abilities to the company. While the length of time for promotions varies greatly from company to company, position to position, and person to person, it is reasonable to expect to wait at least one to three years for your first promotion. In the middle of the hierarchy, a reasonable expectation may be five to ten years between promotions. Toward the top of the hierarchy, it may be reasonable to expect to wait ten or more years between promotions.

SUMMARY

- **(LO 14-1) Discuss the relationship between self-confidence and self-esteem.**
  Self-confidence is being certain and secure about one's own abilities and judgment. Closely related is self-esteem, which is how an individual feels about his or her value as a person. Having high self-esteem can result in a greater sense of self-confidence and vice versa.

- **(LO 14-2) Identify examples of actions necessary for professional advancement.**
  Most people look for ways to advance in their careers as well as develop personally. Workplace strategies that contribute to career success are reinforced by effective negotiation, managing up, self-promotion, and avoiding office politics.

- **(LO 14-3) Describe the importance of having realistic career expectations.**
  Professional workplace expectations must be realistic. No one is *entitled* to career success; it must be earned. Having unrealistic expectations can lead to stress, displeasure with status in a company, or even adverse health effects.

GLOSSARY TERMS

Visit the G-W Learning companion website at **www.g-wlearning.com/careereducation/** to review the following glossary terms.

arrogance   self-confidence

elevator speech   self-esteem

humility   self-image

negotiate   self-promotion

self-awareness

REVIEW

1. Discuss the relationship between self-confidence and self-esteem.

2. What is the distinction between self-confidence and arrogance?

3. Identify examples of workplace strategies that contribute to career success.

4. Explain the concept of self-promoting.

5. Describe the importance of having realistic expectations when entering the workforce.

APPLICATION

1. Describe your personal level of self-confidence. Reflect on a situation or event where self-confidence played a role in your behavior or decision making.

2. Identify a person you think is self-confident. Describe the behaviors this person demonstrates to show his or her confidence level.

3. What do you think your friends or coworkers would say about your level of self-esteem?

4. Describe an arrogant person with whom you have had repeated contact either personally or at your workplace. Make a list of actions and behaviors that this person demonstrates that are translated as arrogant behavior.

5. Explain what the term humility means to you. In what ways do you think that exhibiting humility affects how others perceive you?

6. Identify a person you admire for his or her humility. Explain why you chose this person.

7. Describe how you measure personal career satisfaction.

8. Self-promotion, when handled correctly, can help a person advance in his or her career. An elevator speech is a good strategy to use in situations in which you want to let someone in a decision-making position know who you are and your goals. Write an elevator speech that you could use to promote yourself.

9. Reflect on a work situation where coworkers were involved in office politics. Describe the situation and the outcome of their behavior.

10. Describe your career expectations in both realistic and unrealistic terms.

INTERNET ACTIVITY

Managing Up. The phrase *managing up* is sometimes misinterpreted as negative behavior. Conduct an Internet search for suggestions about how to manage up in an appropriate manner with a supervisor. Make a list of behaviors and activities that you could use in your current job situation.

Realistic Expectations. Having unrealistic expectations about your career can create stress and lead to health problems. Conduct an Internet search for the adverse effects of having unrealistic expectations for a career. Reflect on your own personal expectations for your professional life.

SKILLS PRACTICE

Visit the G-W Learning companion website at **www.g-wlearning.com/careereducation/** to access and complete the following soft skills practice activities:

Activity SS14-1 Self-Confidence. A person's self-confidence is an important factor in career success. Open the SS14-1 file, and review your understanding of self-confidence and arrogance.

Activity SS14-2 Personal SWOT Analysis. A SWOT analysis is a tool you can use to help you understand your strengths, weaknesses, opportunities, and threats. Open the SS14-2 file, and perform a personal SWOT analysis.

APPENDIX A

Punctuation

Terminal Punctuation

In writing, **punctuation** consists of marks used to show the structure of sentences. Punctuation marks used at the end of a sentence are called *terminal punctuation*. Terminal punctuation marks include periods, question marks, and exclamation points.

Periods

A **period** is a punctuation mark used at the end of a declarative sentence. A *declarative sentence* is one that makes a statement. A period signals to the reader that the expressed thought has ended.

> The final exam will be on May 26.
>
> Alma traveled to Lexington to visit her friend.

A period can be used within a quotation. A period should be placed inside a quotation that completes a statement. If a sentence contains a quotation that does not complete the thought, the period should be placed at the end of the sentence, not the end of the quote.

> Jacobi said, "The project is on schedule."
>
> She told me, "Do not let anyone through this door," and she meant it.

Question Marks

A **question mark** is punctuation used at the end of an interrogative sentence. An *interrogative sentence* is one that asks a question. A question mark can be used after a word or sentence that expresses strong emotion, such as shock or doubt.

> Will the plane arrive on time?
>
> What? Are you serious?

A question mark can be part of a sentence that contains a quotation. Place the question mark inside the quotation marks when the quote asks a question. Place the question mark outside the quotation marks if the entire sentence asks a question.

> Teresa asked, "Will the work be finished soon?"
>
> Did he say, "The sale will end on Friday"?

Exclamation Points

An **exclamation point** is a punctuation mark used to express strong emotion. Exclamation points are used at the end of a sentence or after an interjection that stands alone. An exclamation point can be used at the end of a question rather than a question mark, if the writer wishes to show strong emotion.

> Ouch! Stop hurting me!
>
> Will you ever grow up!

As with other terminal punctuation, an exclamation point can be part of a sentence that contains a quotation. Place the exclamation point inside the quotation marks when the quote expresses the strong emotion. Place the exclamation point outside the quotation marks if the entire sentence expresses the strong emotion.

> All of the students shouted, "Hooray!"
>
> She said, "You are disqualified"!

Internal Punctuation

Punctuation marks used within a sentence are called **internal punctuation**. These marks include commas, dashes, parentheses, semicolons, colons, apostrophes, hyphens, and quotation marks.

Commas

A **comma** is a punctuation mark used to separate elements in a sentence. Commas are used to separate items in a series.

> Apple, pears, or grapes will be on the menu.

A comma is used before a coordinating conjunction that joins two independent clauses.

> The sun rose, and the birds began to sing.

Commas are used to separate a nonrestrictive explanatory word or phrase from the rest of the sentence.

> Gloria's husband, Jorge, drove the car.
>
> Yes, I will attend the meeting.

A comma is placed before and after an adverb, such as *however* or *indeed*, when it comes in the middle of a sentence.

> Preparing a delicious meal, however, requires using fresh ingredients.

When an adjective phrase contains coordinate adjectives, use commas to separate the coordinate adjectives. The comma takes the place of the word *and*.

> The *long, hot* summer was finally over.

Commas are used to separate words used in direct address. The words can be proper nouns, the pronoun *you*, or common nouns.

> Quon, please answer the next question.
>
> Everyone, please sit down.

Commas are used to separate elements in dates and addresses. When a date is expressed in the month-day-year format, commas are used to separate the year.

> On December 7, 1941, Japan attacked Pearl Harbor.

When only the month and year or a holiday and year are used, a comma is not needed.

> In January 2010 she retired from her job.

A comma is used after the street address and after the city when an address or location appears in general text.

> Mail the item to 123 Maple Drive, Columbus, OH 43085.

A comma is used to introduce a quotation.

> The speaker attempted to energize the workers by saying, "The only limits are those we put on ourselves."

Dashes and Parentheses

A **dash** is a punctuation mark that separates elements in a sentence or signals an abrupt change in thought. There are two types of dashes: *em dash* and *en dash*. The em dash can be used to replace commas or parentheses to emphasize or set off text. To give emphasis to a break in thought, use an em dash.

> My history teacher—an avid reader—visits the library every week.

The en dash is used as a span or range of numbers, dates, or time.

> We won the baseball game 6–3.
>
> Barack Obama served as President of the United States from 2009–2017.

Parentheses are punctuation marks used to enclose words or phrases that clarify meaning or give added information. Place a period that comes at the end of a sentence inside the parentheses only when the entire sentence is enclosed in parentheses.

> Deliver the materials to the meeting site (the Polluck Building).

Use parentheses to enclose numbers or letters in a list that is part of a sentence.

> Revise the sentences to correct errors in (1) spelling, (2) punctuation, and (3) capitalization.

Semicolons, Colons, and Apostrophes

A **semicolon** is an internal punctuation mark used to separate independent clauses that are similar in thought. A semicolon can also be used to separate items in a series. Typically, items in a series are separated with commas, but if the serial items include commas, a semicolon should be used to avoid confusion.

> Twelve students took the test; two students passed.
>
> We mailed packages to Anchorage, AK; Houston, TX; and Bangor, ME.

A **colon** is an internal punctuation mark that introduces an element in a sentence or paragraph.

> The bag contains three items: a book, a pencil, and an apple.

A colon is also used after a phrase, clause, or sentence that introduces a vertical list.

> Follow these steps:

An **apostrophe** is a punctuation mark used to form possessive words. It is most commonly used in conjunction with the letter *s* to show possession. Position of the apostrophe depends on whether the noun is singular or plural. If singular, place the apostrophe between the noun and the *s*. If plural, place the apostrophe after the *s*.

> Akeno's dress was red.
>
> The students' books were to be put away before the exam.

A **contraction** is a shortened form of a word or term. It is formed by omitting letters from one or more words and replacing them with an apostrophe to create one word—the contraction. An example of a contraction is *it's* for *it is*.

Apostrophes can also be used to indicate that numbers or letters are omitted from words for brevity or writing style.

> Leisure suits were in style in the '60s. (1960s)
>
> The candidates will meet to discuss activities of the gov't. (government)

Hyphens

A **hyphen** is a punctuation mark used to separate parts of compound words, numbers, or ranges. Compound words that always have a hyphen are called **permanent compounds**.

Some adverbs, such as *on-the-job*, always have hyphens.

> The close-up was blurry.
>
> My mother-in-law made dinner.
>
> Their orientation includes on-the-job training.

Compound adjectives have hyphens when they come before the words they modify, but not when they come after them.

> The well-done pot roast was delicious.
>
> The delicious pot roast was well done.
>
> These out-of-date books should be thrown away.
>
> Throw away the books that are out of date.

In some words that have prefixes, a hyphen is used between the prefix and the rest of the word.

> My ex-wife has custody of our children.

When a word is divided at the end of a line of text, a hyphen is used between parts of the word.

> Carter ran down the hall-
> way to answer the door.

Quotation Marks

Quotation marks are used to enclose short, direct quotations and titles of some artistic or written works.

> "Which color do you want," he asked.
>
> "The Raven" is a poem written by Edgar Allan Poe.

A quotation need not be a complete sentence; it can be a word or a phrase as spoken or written by someone. See the examples that follow.

> When the mayor refers to "charitable giving," does that include gifts to all nonprofit organizations?

When writing dialogue, the words of each speaker are enclosed in quotation marks with the appropriate punctuation mark.

> Anna arrived at the office and greeted her coworker, Joan. "Good morning. You're getting an early start today."

Chapter or section titles within complete books, movies, or other artistic work are typically shown in quotation marks. The full title of the work is typically italicized.

> "Books and Journals" is the first chapter in *The Chicago Manual of Style*.

Quotation marks are used to enclose words that are meant to show irony.

> Although Connie had the afternoon off, she was too "busy" to help me.
>
> In a survey of small businesses, one in five managers said their companies are "sinking ships."

APPENDIX B

Capitalization

Capitalization

Capitalization is writing a letter in uppercase (B) rather than lowercase (b). Capital letters signal the beginning of a new sentence and identify important words in titles and headings. Capital letters are also used for proper nouns, for some abbreviations, in personal and professional titles, and for parts of business letters.

A sentence begins with a capital letter. Numbers that begin a sentence should be spelled as words, and the first word should be capitalized.

> Thirty-three students took part in the graduation ceremony.

Capitalize the first, last, and all important words in a heading or title.

> *Gone with the Wind*
>
> *The Adventure of the Hansom Cabs*

For numbers with hyphens in a heading or title, capitalize both words.

> *Twenty-One Candles*

Do not capitalize articles or prepositions within a heading or title unless it is the first word in the title.

> *The Finest Story in the World*

When a title and subtitle are written together, only the first word of the subtitle is capitalized regardless of the part of speech.

> *Presidential Priorities: College's 10th president outlines three campus goals*

Do not capitalize coordinating conjunctions (*yet*, *and*, *but*, *for*, *or*, and *nor*) in a heading or title.

> *Pride and Prejudice*
>
> *Never Marry but for Love*

Do not capitalize parts of names that normally appear in lowercase (Ludwig van Beethoven).

> His favorite composer is Ludwig van Beethoven.

Capitalize the first word in the salutation for a letter.

> Dear Mrs. Stockton:

Capitalize the first word in the complimentary close for a letter.

> Sincerely yours,

Proper nouns begin with a capital letter. Recall that a proper noun is a word that identifies a specific person, place, or thing.

> Joe Wong is the principal of George Rogers Clark High School.

Capitalize initials used in place of names.

> UCLA won the football game.

Capitalize abbreviations that are made up of the first letters of words.

> HTML stands for hypertext markup language.

Months and days, as well as their abbreviations, should be capitalized.

> Mon. is the abbreviation for Monday.

Abbreviations for names of states and countries should be capitalized.

| The price is given in US dollars.

Capitalize abbreviations for directional terms and location terms in street addresses.

| She lives at 123 NW Cedar Ave.

Capitalize call letters of a broadcasting company.

| My favorite television show is on CBS.

Abbreviations that note an era in time should be in capital letters.

| The article included a map of Europe for the year 1200 CE.

Capitalize titles that come before personal names and seniority titles after names.

| Sen. Carl Rogers called Mr. Juarez and Dr. Wang.

| Mr. Thomas O'Malley, Jr., spoke at the ceremony.

Capitalize abbreviations for academic degrees and other professional designations that follow names.

| Jane Patel, LPN, was on duty at the hospital.

APPENDIX C

Number Usage

Number Expression

Numbers can be expressed as figures or as words. In some cases, as in legal documents and on bank checks, numbers are written in both figures and words. When the two expressions of a number do not agree, readers are alerted to ask for clarification.

Number expression guidelines are not as widely agreed upon as rules for punctuation and capitalization. Follow the guidelines in this section for general writing. If you are writing a research report or an article for a particular group or publication, ask whether there are number expression guidelines you should follow for that item.

Numbers Expressed as Words

In general writing, use words for numbers one through nine.

> One dog and three cats sat on the porch.

Use figures for numbers 10 and greater. (See other style guides for exceptions to this guideline.)

> She placed an order for 125 blue ink pens.

When some numbers in a sentence are 9 or less and some are 10 or greater, write all the numbers as figures.

> The box contains 5 books, 10 folders, and 15 pads of paper.

Use words for numbers that are indefinite or approximate amounts.

> About fifty people signed the petition.

Use words for numbers one through nine followed by *million*, *billion*, and so forth. For numbers 10 or greater followed by *million*, *billion*, and so forth, use a figure and the word.

> Two million people live in this region.

> By 2016, the population of the United States had grown to over 300 million.

When a number begins a sentence, use words instead of figures. If the number is long when written as words, consider revising the sentence so it does not begin with a number.

> Twenty copies of the report were prepared.

When two numbers come together in a sentence, use words for one of the numbers.

> On the bus, there were 15 ten-year-olds.

Use words for numbers with *o'clock* to express time.

> Come to my house for lunch at eleven o'clock.

Use figures with *a.m.* and *p.m.* to express time.

> The assembly will begin at 9:30 a.m.

To express amounts of money, use figures with a currency sign.

> The total amount is $18,395.40.

Do not use a decimal and two zeros when all dollar amounts in a sentence are whole amounts.

> The charges were $5, $312, and $89.

For an isolated amount less than $1, use figures and the word *cents*.

> Buy a cup of lemonade for 75 cents.

When an amount less than $1 appears with other amounts greater than $1, use figures and dollar signs for all of the numbers.

| The prices were $12.50, $0.89, and $12.45.

For a large, whole dollar amount, use the dollar sign, a figure, and a word, such as *million* or *billion*.

| The profits for last year were $5 million.

Days and years in dates should be identified with figures.

| On February 19, 2015, the court was not in session.

Use words for fractions. Note that a hyphen is placed between the words.

| Place one-half of the mixture in the pan.

Use figures for mixed numbers (a whole number and a fraction).

| I bought 3 1/2 yards of red fabric.

When writing a number with decimals, use figures.

| The measurements are 1.358 and 0.878.

Use figures in measurements, such as distance, weight, and percentages.

| We drove 258 miles today.

| The winning pumpkin weighs 50 pounds.

| Sales have increased 20 percent in the last year.

Pages, chapters, figures, or parts in a book should be referenced with figures.

| Open your book to chapter 3, page 125.

| Refer to figure 6 on page 72 for an example.

Glossary

A

active listening. Fully participating as an individual processes what a person says. (9)

arrogance. Attitude in which an individual believes he or she is better than other people. (14)

attitude. How personal thoughts or feelings affect a person's outward behavior. (1)

B

background check. Investigation into personal data about a job applicant (11).

behavioral questions. Interview questions that draw on an individual's previous experiences and decisions. (11)

bias-free words. Neutral words that impart neither a positive nor negative message. (6)

block style letter. Letter formatted so all lines are flush with the left margin and no indentations are used. (10)

body language. Nonverbal messages sent through gestures, facial expressions, and posture. (7)

business-casual dress. Dress that is often considered to be "one step down" from business-professional dress. (5)

business-professional dress. Most formal style of dress in the workplace. (5)

C

channel. How the message is transmitted; also known as *medium*. (6)

code of ethics. Document that dictates how business should be conducted. (2)

collaboration skills. Behaviors that individuals exhibit when working with others to achieve a common goal and maintain working relationships. (12)

communication. Process of using words, sounds, signs, or actions to exchange information and express thoughts. (6)

communication process. Series of actions on the part of the sender and the receiver of a message, as well as the path the message follows. (6)

confidentiality. Specific information that is never shared, except with those who have clearance to receive it. (2)

conflict. Strong disagreement between two or more people or a difference that prevents agreement. (12)

conflict management. Process of recognizing and resolving disputes. (12)

conflict-resolution skills. Skills required to resolve a situation in which a disagreement could lead to hostile behavior such as shouting or fighting. (12)

connotation. Word's meaning apart from what it explicitly names or describes. (6)

constructive criticism. Criticism offered in a friendly manner with the objective of improving outcome and performance of another person. (3)

context. Environment in which something occurs or the surrounding information that is communicated. (6)

cover message. Letter or e-mail sent with a résumé to introduce the applicant and summarize his or her reasons for applying for a job. (11)

critical-thinking skills. Skills that provide the ability to analyze and interpret a situation and make reasonable judgment and decisions. (3)

cultural awareness. Understanding of the differences and similarities between one's personal culture and the culture of another person or group. (13)

cultural competency. Acknowledgment of cultural differences and the ability to adapt one's communication style to successfully send and receive messages despite those differences. (13)

cultural intelligence. Ability to adapt to unfamiliar cultural situations; often abbreviated as *CQ*. (13)

culture. Shared beliefs, customs, practices, and social behaviors of a particular group. (13)

cyberbullying. Using electronic technology to harass or threaten an individual. (2)

D

decoding. Process of translating a message. (6)

digital citizenship. Standard of appropriate behavior when using technology. (2)

disability. Physical or mental impairment that substantially limits one or more of a person's major life activities. (13)

diversity. Having representatives from different backgrounds, cultures, or demographics in a group. (13)

Note: The number in parentheses following each definition indicates the chapter in which the term can be found.

E

elevator speech. Several sentences that tell who a person is, what he or she does that is of value, and why that work is important. (14)

emotional control. Process of directing one's feelings and reactions toward a desirable result that is socially acceptable. (3)

emotional intelligence quotient (EQ). Ability of a person to perceive emotions in one's self and in others and use this information to guide social behavior. (1)

empathy. Having the ability to share someone else's emotions. (1)

employability skills. Skills that help an individual find a job, perform well in the workplace, and gain success in a job or career. (1)

employment verification. Process through which the information provided on an applicant's résumé is checked to verify that it is correct. (11)

encoding. Process of turning the idea for a message into symbols that can be communicated. (6)

English as a Second Language (ESL). Field of education concerned with teaching English to those whose native language is not English; also known as *English as a Foreign Language (EFL)*. (13)

enunciation. Clearly and distinctly pronouncing syllables and sounds. (7)

ethics. Moral principles or beliefs that direct a person's behavior. (2)

ethnicity. Culture with which a person identifies. (13)

etiquette. Art of using good manners in any situation. (2)

euphemism. Word that expresses unpleasant ideas in more pleasant terms. (6)

F

feedback. Receiver's response to the sender. (6)

Form I-9 Employment Eligibility Verification. Employment form used to verify an employee's identity and that he or she is authorized to work in the United States. (11)

G

generation. Group of people who were born and lived during the same time period. (13)

goal. Something to be achieved in a specified time period. (3)

group discussion. Speaking situation in which three or more individuals share their ideas about a subject. (7)

group dynamics. Interacting forces within a group or team, including the attitudes, behaviors, and personalities of all members. (12)

H

hard skills. Critical skills necessary to perform the required work-related tasks of a position. (1)

hearing. Physical process of sound waves reaching a person's ears, which send signals to his or her brain. (9)

humility. To be modest and not to think one is better than other people. (14)

hypothetical questions. Interview questions that require a candidate to imagine a situation and describe how he or she would act. (11)

I

image. Perception others have of a person based on that person's dress, behavior, and speech. (1)

impromptu speaking. Talking without advance notice or an opportunity to plan what will be said. (7)

inclusion. Practice of recognizing, accepting, valuing, and respecting diversity. (13)

intellectual property. Something that comes from a person's mind, such as an idea, invention, or process. (2)

intercultural communication. Process of sending and receiving messages between people of various cultures. (13)

intonation. Rise and fall in the pitch of an individual's voice. (7)

introduction. Making a person known to someone else by sharing the person's name and other relevant information. (8)

J

jargon. Technical terminology or vocabulary specific to a field of work or group. (6)

L

leadership. Ability to influence others to reach a goal. (12)

libel. Publishing a false statement about someone that causes others to have a bad or untrue opinion of him or her. (2)

listening. Intellectual process that combines hearing with evaluating. (9)

M

mediation. Inclusion of a neutral person, called a *mediator*, to help the conflicting parties resolve their dispute and reach an agreement. (12)

mock interview. Practice interview conducted with another person. (11)

modified block style letter. Letter formatted with the date, complimentary close, and signature to the right of the center point of the letter and all other elements are flush with the left margin. (10)

modulation. Changing the emphasis of words by raising and lowering the voice. (7)

morals. Individual's ideas of what is right and wrong. (2)

multigenerational workforce. Workforce that consists of employees who represent multiple age groups and generations. (13)

N

negotiate. Formal discussion between two or more people in an attempt to reach an agreement. (14)

negotiation. When individuals involved in a conflict come together to discuss a compromise. (12)

networking. Talking with people an individual knows and developing new relationships that can lead to potential career or job opportunities. (1)

nonverbal communication. Any action, behavior, or attitude that sends a message to the receiver. (7)

P

paralanguage. Attitude projected with the tone and pitch of a person's voice. (7)

parliamentary procedure. Process for holding meetings so that they are orderly and democratic. (8)

passive listening. Casually listening to someone talk. (9)

personal information management (PIM). System that individuals use to acquire, organize, maintain, retrieve, and use information. (3)

piracy. Unethical and illegal copying or downloading of software, files, and other protected material. (2)

pitch. Highness or lowness of a sound. (7)

plagiarism. Claiming another person's material as one's own, which is both unethical and illegal. (2)

portfolio. Selection of related materials that are collected and organized to show the qualifications, skills, and talents that support an individual's career or personal goals. (11)

problem solving. Process of choosing a course of action after evaluating available information and weighing the costs, benefits, and consequences of alternative actions. (3)

professional attire. Dress that is dictated by the workplace and appropriate for the job. (5)

professional image. Image an individual projects in the professional world. (1)

professional network. Group of professionals a person knows and who know the person. (1)

professionalism. Act of exhibiting appropriate character, judgment, and behavior by a person who is trained to perform a job. (1)

proprietary information. Anything that is owned by a business. (2)

protocol. Set of customs and rules that explains appropriate conduct or procedures in formal situations. (4)

public speaking. Communication delivered to a large group from a podium and with a microphone; also known as *public communication*. (7)

R

reference. Person who knows an applicant's skills, talents, or personal traits and is willing to recommend him or her. (11)

resilience. Person's ability to cope with and recover from change or adversity. (1)

résumé. Document that profiles a person's career goals, education, and work history. (11)

S

self-awareness. Sense of being aware of one's feelings, behaviors, needs, and other elements that make up the whole person. (14)

self-confidence. Being certain and secure about one's own abilities and judgment. (14)

self-esteem. How an individual feels about his or her value as a person. (14)

self-image. Way a person thinks about himself or herself, including personal abilities, appearance, and other people's perception. (14)

self-management skills. Skills that enable an individual to control and make the best use of his or her time and abilities. (3)

self-promotion. Act of making coworkers, peers, managers, or potential employers aware of oneself so that personal value can be established. (14)

skill. Something an individual does well. (1)

slander. Speaking a false statement about someone that causes others to have a bad opinion of him or her. (2)

SMART goals. Goals that are specific, measurable, attainable, realistic, and timely. (3)

social responsibility. Behaving with sensitivity to social, environmental, and economic issues. (2)

soft skills. Skills used to communicate and work well with others. (1)

Standard English. English language usage that follows accepted rules for word use, pronunciation, spelling, grammar, and punctuation. (6)

stereotype. Belief or generalization about a group of people with a given set of characteristics. (13)

stress. Body's reaction to increased demands or dangerous situations. (3)

stress-management skills. Skills that enable an individual to identify and control stress. (3)

T

team. Group of two or more people who work together to achieve a common goal. (12)

teamwork. Cooperative efforts by individual team members to achieve a goal. (12)

time management. Practice of organizing time and work assignments to increase personal efficiency. (3)

tone. Impression of the overall content of the message. (6)

transmission. Act of sending a message. (6)

U

uniform. Prescribed form of dress worn by everybody in a particular group, such as a company or department. (5)

V

verbal communication process. Series of actions on the part of the sender and the receiver of a message. (7)

W

work ethic. Principle that honest work is its own reward. (2)

work-life balance. Amount of time spent at work compared to the amount of time spent with family and friends and engaged in leisure activities. (13)

workplace bullying. Intentional, repeated mistreatment of a person by another person using verbal abuse, threats, or any other action that prevents a person from doing his or her job without fear. (2)

workspace etiquette. Applying the rules of good manners while a person is in his or her own workspace and the workspaces of others. (4)

Index

A

acceptable use policy, 13
active listening, 73
   listen to instructions, 75
   persuasive talk, 76
   requests, 75
   specific information, 75
   types, 74
adjourning, 113
age, 123–124
   communication, 124
   cultural expectations, 124
   stereotypes, 124
Age Discrimination in Employment
   Act, 123
age-neutral, 123
aggressive behavior, 113
Americans with Disabilities Act
   (ADA), 122
application process, 99–100
   applying in person, 100
   applying online, 100
arrogance, 134–135
assertive behavior, 113
attire, 37–44
   business meeting apparel, 40–41
   inappropriate apparel for the
      workplace, 41
   workplace dress, 38–40
   uniforms, 38
attitude, 4
audience, 46
autocratic leadership style, 116

B

background check, 105
barrier, 47
behavioral questions, 102
benefits, 139
bias, 124
bias-free words, 49
block style letter, 84
body language, 56–58
   definition, 56
brown-nosing, 137
Bryant, Paul William "Bear", 136
Buffet, Warren, 23

bullying, 115
Bush, Lauren, 13
business-casual dress, 39
business dining, 32–33
business dining etiquette, 32
business meeting apparel, 40–41
business-professional dress, 38
business protocol, 29

C

career-appropriate dress. *See*
   workplace dress
career ladder, 138
Case Study,
   communication skills, 48
   diversity, 125
   humility, 136
   listening with purpose, 76
   professional image, 4
   résumé fraud, 99
   social responsibility, 13
   speaking, 64
   team conflict, 115
   thank-you note, 88
   time management, 23
   verbal communication, 58
   workplace dress code, 40
   workplace etiquette, 30
channel, 46
citation guidelines. *See* intellectual
   property
Civil Rights Act of 1964, 122
code of conduct, 10
code of ethics, 10
collaboration skills, 112
committee. *See* cross-functional
   team
communication, 46–47, 124
   barriers, 47
   communication process,
      46–47
   definition, 46
   in the workplace, 124
   purposes of, 46
communication barriers, 47
   receiving barrier, 47
   sending barrier, 47
communication process, 46

communication skills, 45–52
   communication, 46–47
   language, 47–49
confidence, 133–142
   professional success, 135–137
   realistic expectations, 138–139
   self-confidence, 134–135
confidentiality, 11
conflict, 113
conflict management, 113
conflict-resolution skills, 114
connotation, 48
constructive criticism, 20
context, 48
copyleft, 15
copyright, 14
cover message, 94, 96
CQ. *See* cultural intelligence
Creative Commons (CC) license, 15
critical-thinking skills, 21
criticism, 20
cross-functional team, 112
cultural awareness, 125–126
cultural background. *See* personal
   space
cultural competency, 127
cultural expectations, 124
cultural intelligence, 126–127
cultural sensitivity, 126
culture, 121, 124–127
   careful listening, 128
   clear speech, 128
   cultural awareness, 125–126
   cultural competency, 127
   cultural intelligence, 126–127
   definition, 121
   nonverbal communication, 128
cyberbullying, 12

D

decision-making process, 21
decoding, 47
democratic leadership style, 116
difficult people, 114–116
digital citizenship, 12–15
   copyrights, 14–15
   definition, 12
   intellectual property, 14

digital devices, 32
digital footprint, 12
direct reports, 138
disability, 122
diversity, 120–132
 benefits of, 129
 culture, 124–127
 definition, 121
 high productivity, 129
 improved customer service, 129
 in the workplace, 121–124
 intercultural communication,
   127–128
 new ideas, 129
 reputation, 129
documentation of identity, 106

E

elevator speech, 137
e-mail, 87–88
emotional control, 20
Emotional Intelligence Quotient
   (EQ), 3, 20
empathize, 78
empathy, 3
employable skills, 3
employment,
 application process, 99–100
 preparing for interview,
   100–103
 writing and interviewing,
   93–110
employment forms, 105–106
 benefits forms, 106
 Form I-9, 105–106
 Form W-4, 106
employment verification, 105
encoding, 46
English as a Foreign Language
   (EFL), 127
English as a Second Language
   (ESL), 127
enunciation, 55
ethical communication, 11–12
 confidentiality, 11–12
 social responsibility, 12
ethics, 9–18
 definition, 10
 digital citizenship, 12–15
 ethical communication,
   11–12
ethnicity, 121

etiquette, 12, 28–36
 business dining, 32–33
 definition, 29
 digital devices, 32
 funerals, 33
 workspace, 30–32
euphemism, 49

F

fair use doctrine, 15
false advertising, 11
feedback, 47
flaming, 13
Form I-9 Employment Eligibility
   Verification, 105
Form W-2 Wage and Tax
   Statement, 106
Form W-4 Employee's Withholding
   Allowance Certificate, 106
formal communication, 46
formal language, 47
formal meetings, 77–79
 arrive early, 77
 effective note-taking, 77–78
 fight external distractions and
   barriers, 78
 friendly questions, 78
 provide feedback, 78–79
 sit in the front, 77
 unfriendly questions, 79
for-purchase. *See* software licenses
freeware. *See* software licenses
functional team, 112
funerals, 33

G

gender discrimination, 121
gender expression, 121
gender identity, 121
generation, 123
GNU General Public License (GNU
   GPL), 15
goal, 22
goal setting, 22–23
 attainable, 23
 long-term, 22
 measurable, 22
 realistic, 23
 short-term, 22
 specific, 22
 timely, 23

go-getter, 127
group discussion, 56
group dynamics, 113, 123
group member roles, 112
group process, 113
group-development process, 113

H

haggling. *See* cultural
   intelligence
haptics communication, 57
hard skills, 2
hearing, 73
hiring process, 105–106
 employee checks, 105
 employment forms, 105–106
humility, 135
hypothetical questions, 101

I

image, 5
impromptu speaking, 55
inclusion, 121
informal communication, 46
informal language, 48
infringement, 14
intellectual property, 14
intercultural communication, 127
Internet etiquette, workplace
   disruptions, 36
interpersonal communication, 56
interpersonal skills, 3
interpreter. *See* cultural
   competency
interview,
 appropriate attire, 103
 behavioral questions, 102
 evaluation, 104
 hypothetical questions,
   101–102
 interview process has ended,
   104
 mock interview, 101
 preparing for, 100–103
 questions, 101
 questions employers should not
   ask, 102
 questions to ask employer,
   102–103
 thank-you message, 104
intonation, 54

introductions, 63–65
   definition, 63
   introducing others, 63
   introducing speakers, 64–65
   introducing yourself, 63
Issacs, Cheryl Boone, 48

J

jargon, 49
job application, 100
job-specific skills, 2
Jobs, Steve, 115

L

laissez-faire leadership style, 116
language, 47–49
   biased words, 49
   condescending words, 49
   euphemisms, 49
   jargon and clichés, 49
leadership, 116
leadership skills, 116
leadership styles, 116
letters, 84–86
libel, 11
license, 15
licensing agreement, 15
LinkedIn, 5
listening, 73, 128
listening process, 73–74
   show attention, 74
   types of listening, 73
listening skills, 72–82
   formal meetings, 77–79
   listen with purpose, 74–76
   listening process, 73–74

M

manage up, 136–137
mediation, 114
mediator, 114
medium. *See* channel
meetings, 67–68
   guidelines for effective meetings, 67
   remote meetings, 68
message, 46
mock interview, 101
modified block style letter, 84
modulation, 54
morals, 10

multigenerational workforce, 123
multiracial. *See* race and ethnicity
Muñoz, Anthony, 64

N

negativity, 20
negotiate, 135
negotiation, 114
netiquette, 12, 87
networking, 5
networking site, 5
nonverbal communication, 56–58
   body language, 56
   definition, 56
   eye contact, 57
   paralanguage, 58
   personal space, 57
   touch, 57

O

office politics, 137
open source, 15

P

paralanguage, 58
parliamentary procedure, 67
passive behavior, 113
passive listening, 73
people skills, 3
personal information management (PIM), 22
personal space, 57
piracy, 14
pitch, 54
plagiarism, 14
playing up, 137
portfolio, 97–98
   portfolio elements, 98
positive attitude, 4–5
positive stereotypes, 123
problem solving, 20–21
professional attire, 38
professional etiquette, 29
professional image, 5
professionalism, 1–8
   definition, 2
   image of a professional, 5
   positive attitude, 4–5
   skills of a professional, 2–3
professional network, 5

professional success, 135–137
   manage up, 136–137
   negotiation, 135
   office politics, 137
   self-promotion, 137
promotion, 139
proprietary information, 12
protocol, 29
public domain, 15
public speaking, 56

R

race and ethnicity, 121–122
Reagan, President Ronald, 88
realistic expectations, 138–139
   benefits, 139
   position, 138
   promotion, 139
   salary, 138–139
real-time video conferencing, 68
receiving barrier, 47
reference, 98
resilience, 5
résumé, 94–95
Robert's Rules of Order, 67
Rowling, J.K., 76
RSVP, 89

S

salary, 138–139
self-awareness, 137
self-confidence, 134–135
   definition, 135
self-esteem, 134
self-image, 134
self-management skills, 19–27
   definition, 20
   developing, 20–23
   emotional control, 20
   goal-setting, 22–23
   problem-solving, 20–21
   stress-management skills, 23
   time management, 21–22
self-promotion, 137
self-talk, 134
sender, 46
sending barrier, 47
shareware. *See* software licenses
skill, 2
slander, 11

small group communication. *See* group discussion
SMART goals, 22
social media etiquette, 89
social responsibility, 12
soft skills, 3
software licenses, 15
Sotomayor, Sonia, 125
spamming, 13
speaking skills, 62–71
    introductions, 63–65
    leading a meeting, 67–68
    telephone calls, 65–67
Standard English, 47
stereotype, 121
stress, 24
stress-management skills, 24
stress-management strategies, 23
summarizing, 75

T

task force. *See* cross-functional team
teams, 111–119
    conflict resolution, 113–114
    definition, 112
    difficult people, 114–116
    group dynamics, 113
    in the workplace, 112–113
    leadership, 116
teamwork, 112
telephone calls, 65–67
    leaving voice mail messages, 66–67
    placing, 66
    receiving, 65–66

telephone etiquette, 65
terms of use, 14
thank-you message, after an interview, 104
thank-you notes, 89
Thompson, Scott, 99
time management, 21–22
tone, 48, 54
trade secret, 12
transgender. *See* diversity
transmission, 46
Tuckman, Bruce, 113
Tutu, Desmond, 58

U

uniform, 38

V

verbal communication, 54–56
    common errors in pronunciation, 55
    speaking situations, 55–56
    voice, 54
    words, 54
verbal communication process, 54
voice mail messages, leaving, 66–67

W

Walmart, employee dress code, 40
Williams, Brian, 4
Williams, Serena, 30

work ethic, 10
workforce, benefits of diversity, 129
work-life balance, 124
workplace,
    age, 123–124
    definition, 30
    diversity in, 121–124
    gender, 121
    race, 121–122
    teams in, 112–113
    teamwork, 112
    workplace culture, 124
workplace bullying, 11
workplace dress, 38–40
    business-casual dress, 39
    business-professional dress, 38–39
    jeans day, 39–40
    uniforms, 38
workplace ethics, 10
work-related tasks, 2
workspace, 30–32
    cubicles, 31–32
    offices, 31
    shared spaces, 32
    workspace etiquette, 30
writing etiquette, 84–89
    e-mail, 87–88
    letters, 84–86
    RSVP, 89
    thank-you notes, 89
written communication, 83–92
    social media etiquette, 89
    writing etiquette, 84–89